Interface Programming
in SAP® ABAP

Dr. Boris Rubarth

Thank you for purchasing this book from Espresso Tutorials!

Like a cup of espresso coffee, Espresso Tutorials SAP books are concise and effective. We know that your time is valuable and we deliver information in a succinct and straightforward manner. It only takes our readers a short amount of time to consume SAP concepts. Our books are well recognized in the industry for leveraging tutorial-style instruction and videos to show you step by step how to successfully work with SAP.

Check out our YouTube channel to watch our videos at
https://www.youtube.com/user/EspressoTutorials.

If you are interested in SAP Finance and Controlling, join us at
http://www.fico-forum.com/forum2/
to get your SAP questions answered and contribute to discussions.

Related titles from Espresso Tutorials:

▶ Jelena Perfiljeva: What on Earth is an SAP® IDoc?
  http://5130.espresso-tutorials.com

▶ Michal Krawczyk: SAP® SOA Integration –
  Enterprise Service Monitoring
  http://5077.espresso-tutorials.com

▶ Tom Zamir: Using SAP® BRFplus in Big Data Scenarios
  http://5256.espresso-tutorials.com

▶ Thomas Stutenbäumer: Practical Guide to ABAP®.
  Part 1: Conceptual Design, Development, Debugging
  http://5121.espresso-tutorials.com

▶ Thomas Stutenbäumer: Practical Guide to ABAP®.
  Part 2: Performance, Enhancements, Transports
  http://5138.espresso-tutorials.com

Dr. Boris Rubarth
Interface Programming in SAP® ABAP

ISBN:	978-1-72290-294-0
Editor:	Tracey Duffy
Cover Design:	Philip Esch
Cover Photo:	© psdesign1, # 68900453 – stock.adobe.com
Interior Book Design:	Johann-Christian Hanke

All rights reserved.

1st edition 2018, revised print 2020

© 2020 by Espresso Tutorials GmbH, Gleichen

URL: *www.espresso-tutorials.com*

Feedback
We greatly appreciate any kind of feedback you have concerning this book. Please mail us at *info@espresso-tutorials.com*.

Table of Contents

Preface

This book, *Interface Programming in SAP ABAP*, offers an easy and straightforward path into the world of ABAP interfaces. It introduces all relevant technologies for system-to-system communication using ABAP.

There is a wide variety of interface technologies available and this sometimes makes things confusing. However, this wide variety of technologies offers solutions for all kinds of scenarios, which is what makes it so fascinating. I wrote this book to help you dive smoothly into the details of these technologies.

Why are we still using RFC, even though all state-of-the-art business systems can handle Web services? What is the benefit of asynchronous communication if it does not provide an immediate answer? If you are looking for answers to questions like these, this book is for you.

The stages of this journey through all relevant ABAP interface technologies build on one another. They establish an example application that you implement and extend to gain practical experience with the technologies.

Throughout the journey, you will pass through stations you may already know, see aspects which seem to be clear, but which may be highlighted from a different angle. Therefore, I invite you to follow the journey from the beginning to the end, even if the path seems quite easy during the first steps.

To help you understand the explanations given in this book, you do need some prior knowledge of ABAP, so you should be familiar at least with the concepts outlined in *First Steps in ABAP* (Dr. Boris Rubarth, Espresso Tutorials, 2013). You also need access to two ABAP systems (or at least two clients in one system) to work through the exercises.

After reading this book, you will be able to decide which interface technology to choose for your project and you will be able to start the implementation immediately.

Download all code listings

 To access all of the source code referenced in this book, visit *https://de.espresso-tutorials.com/_ABAP_P3.php*.

This book is dedicated to my beloved wife. Without her support and charitableness, this book would not have been possible. A special thank you goes to the great team at Espresso Tutorials for their comprehensive and flexible support.

We have added a few icons to highlight important information. These include:

Tips

 Tips highlight information that provides more details about the subject being described and/or additional background information.

Examples

 Examples help illustrate a topic better by relating it to real world scenarios.

> **Attention**
>
> Attention notices highlight information that you should be aware of when you go through the examples in this book on your own.

Finally, a note concerning the copyright: all screenshots printed in this book are the copyright of SAP SE. All rights are reserved by SAP SE. Copyright pertains to all SAP images in this publication. For the sake of simplicity, we do not mention this specifically underneath every screen-shot.

1 Using Remote Function Call (RFC)

Understanding the RFC protocol is important not only for creating applications using this versatile and well-established communication technique; with the remote-enabled function modules it is also an important foundation for modern interfaces, such as Web services, in ABAP.

Our journey starts with the creation of an RFC in three minutes. We then extend the example and add missing parts. The journey introduces both the client and server in parallel and gradually becomes more comprehensive, ultimately leading to our own scenario.

1.1 Implementing an RFC in three minutes

Let us assume that you are developing an ABAP application which requires data provided by a function module that resides in another ABAP system. Obtaining this data is quite easy: you use a *Remote Function Call (RFC)*. Figure 1.1 shows a simplified view of the principle.

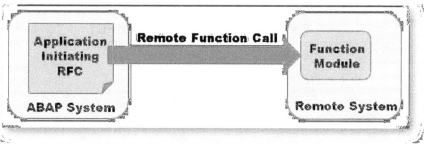

Figure 1.1: Simplified view of a Remote Function Call

Your application initiates the RFC and the remote system provides the function module.

If you are familiar with the ABAP statement `CALL FUNCTION`, you simply use the addition `DESTINATION` and your (local) function call becomes an RFC statement:

```
CALL FUNCTION '<NAME_OF_FUNCTION_MODULE>'
DESTINATION '<NAME_OF_DESTINATION>'
```

The addition `DESTINATION` references an RFC destination that holds the information for connecting to the server. We will look at this configuration part of the story shortly.

Because your ABAP application initiates the call, it is the RFC client. The remote ABAP system on which the function module resides acts as an RFC server.

1. The client initiates the communication and sends the request.

2. The server picks up the request and passes it to the respective function module.

3. The server then returns the response from the function module back to the client via the existing connection, as depicted in Figure 1.2. Therefore, the server does not need an RFC destination to provide the response to the client.

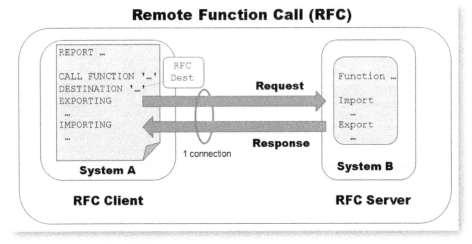

Figure 1.2: RFC client-server view

Communication terminology

 As we progress through our journey of developing an interface, we will not only build development knowledge but also gain an understanding of relevant terminology.

Figure 1.2 shows the *client* and *server* parts of an RFC and both have a *communication interface*. An *interface* is the technical capability of an application system to exchange data with other systems or applications. The interface comprises both parts of a data exchange: the *request* and the *response*.

A first simplified example of a report with an RFC may look as shown in Listing 1.1:

```
REPORT z_rfc_in_three_minutes.

DATA: gs_rfcsi TYPE rfcsi, gv_dest.

CALL FUNCTION 'RFC_SYSTEM_INFO'
DESTINATION gv_dest
  IMPORTING
     rfcsi_export              = gs_rfcsi
*    CURRENT_RESOURCES         =
*    MAXIMAL_RESOURCES         =
*    RECOMMENDED_DELAY         =
            .
WRITE gs_rfcsi-rfcdbsys.
```

Listing 1.1: Report Z_RFC_IN_THREE_MINUTES

The example seems OK and it even works—but this is neither a real Remote Function Call nor proper coding. We cheated in several aspects.

Let's start with the remote system: *remote* means an ABAP client (or system) different to the one in which the *RFC client application* was executed. The example above used a variable gv_dest with the same content as SPACE which executes the function module locally. Check the content of rfchost and rfcsysid in the structure gs_rfcsi, as they are indicators for this. Therefore, to create a Remote Function Call, we have to create an RFC destination that points to a remote system: either another ABAP system or at least another ABAP client in the same system. Once we have done this in Section 1.2, we will discuss other aspects for improving this simplified coding example.

Conventions for program-internal names

We will follow the naming conventions provided by SAP, as listed in the ABAP documentation. These naming conventions can be found on the Help Portal. For SAP_BASIS 7.50, see: *https://help.sap.com/doc/abapdocu_750_index_ htm/7.50/en-US/abennaming_conventions.htm*.

1.2   Creating RFC destinations (to ABAP systems)

You define your *RFC destination* in transaction SM59. We will provide only a simple example, as maintenance of RFC destinations is typically the task of a system administrator and not a developer.

In transaction SM59, click CREATE. On the maintenance screen that appears, enter the name for your destination (use upper case), choose connection type *3* (for an ABAP target system), and enter a short text (required!)—here, *ABAP Connection*. Now press `Enter` to adapt the parameters shown for the requirements of a target system of type ABAP, as shown in the middle image in Figure 1.3.

On the TECHNICAL SETTINGS tab, select LOAD BALANCING to allow the target system to decide which server to use (instead of specifying a dedicated one yourself)—this is the recommended practice. In the TARGET SYSTEM field, enter the target system ID. In the MSG. SERVER field, enter the target host name, and in the GROUP field, enter an existing logon group in the target system (SPACE always exists).

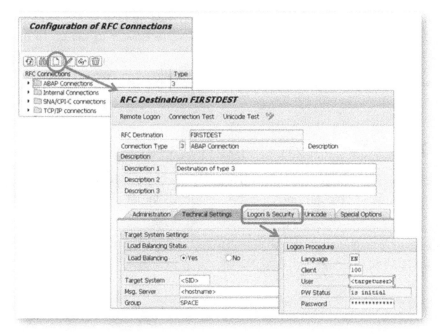

Figure 1.3: Creating an RFC destination of type 3

Switch to the LOGON & SECURITY tab and enter the target ABAP client. Save the settings and click CONNECTION TEST. If the test is successful, you can use the destination in your program. If you do not provide a target system user (and password) and leave these fields empty, the target system will display a logon screen later during the call in which the destination is used in an application.

Destination independent of the target function module

 As you have seen, the configuration of an RFC destination does not point to one specific function module. The destination is generic for the server system and can be used from within different RFC client applications (but from all ABAP clients of the system). Note that *ABAP client* is not the same as *client application*: an ABAP system typically has several ABAP clients with separate business data, whereas a client application connects to an RFC server.

If you have maintained a valid target system user of type *Dialog* (and the password for this user), you can click REMOTE LOGON to log on to the target system directly with that user.

Note that if you have not provided a user in the RFC destination, your client application (using this destination) cannot be used for background processing.

Of course, you never use a fixed name for the RFC destination in your code. Change requests (for transporting development objects along the development landscape) do not include RFC destinations (which are configuration objects) because the respective target system will require different connection data.

Listing 1.2 shows the improved version of report Z_RFC_IN_THREE_ MINUTES.

```
REPORT z_rfc_in_three_minutes.

DATA: gs_rfcsi TYPE rfcsi.
PARAMETERS:
pa_dest TYPE rfcdes-rfcdest DEFAULT 'FIRSTDEST'.

CALL FUNCTION 'RFC_SYSTEM_INFO'
DESTINATION pa_dest
 IMPORTING
    rfcsi_export              = gs_rfcsi
*   CURRENT_RESOURCES         =
*   MAXIMAL_RESOURCES         =
*   RECOMMENDED_DELAY         =
            .
WRITE gs_rfcsi-rfcdbsys.
```

Listing 1.2: Improved report Z_RFC_IN_THREE_MINUTES

The advantage of referencing `rfcdes-rfcdest` for the parameter is that an F4 help is provided on the selection screen.

18

Predefined destinations 'NONE' and 'BACK'

 The predefined destination *'NONE'* is like using a variable with content equal to SPACE: the call still passes through the local gateway (this is explained later in Section 1.7).

'BACK' is a destination that you can use inside function modules to call back to the respective client system. Special security considerations for this destination are required and are possible with a *callback whitelist*. See SAP Note 1686632 for details.

Transaction SM59 lists 'BACK' and 'NONE' under INTERNAL CONNECTIONS. In your application, you have to reference them as strings, that is, inside single inverted commas (in contrast to SPACE, which is an ABAP variable).

As already stated, no destination is required in the server system to receive or respond to a call. However, some configuration is required in the server system to enable RFC communication in general, and this involves more than providing a user which can be specified in the RFC destination. Therefore, let us take a little time to check the RFC requirements for the target system.

1.3   Considering target system configuration

It is obvious that the function module to be invoked must already exist in the target system. You also need a valid user, as already discussed.

Restrict access to destinations that contain the logon user

 The client system will use the user/password information from the destination (if provided) for the logon to the server system. This user is different to the logon user that you used to log on to the client system. The field AUTHORIZATION FOR DESTINATION allows you to restrict which logon users can use the RFC destination with the user enclosed in the destination. For example, the system should not be set up such that all logon users can use a destination that is capable of changing salary statements in the target system—unfortunately.

When setting up communication between systems, your administrator should consider the following two aspects:

1. Setting up *secure network communication (SNC)* secures the communication between the systems (via data encryption).

2. It is also possible to create a *trusting/trusted RFC connection* between ABAP systems which allows users to log on without a password and also allows single sign-on across system boundaries.

The target system user requires some authorizations in the target system. One generic requirement references the *authorization object* S_RFC for the respective function module to be called. It requires activity 16 for execution—Figure 1.4 shows an example for an authorization object which allows you to call the function module RFC_SYSTEM _INFO.

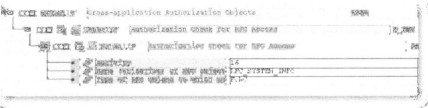

Figure 1.4: Example of authorization for object S_RFC

Application-specific authorizations are also required, to pass the authorization checks executed within the function module coding.

Several destinations, different user, type Communication

 Regardless of your situation, you should use a target system user of type *Communication* with restricted authorizations in the target system. It is also good practice to have several, client application-specific destinations with respective application-specific users and authorizations: if one user is locked for any reason, this will ensure that some RFC destinations can still be used.

This is especially relevant if several client systems connect to the same server system. If they all use the same user, and one of the client applications locks the user (wrong password and too many failed logon attempts), all other client systems are affected.

We have already mentioned in Section 1.2 that the RFC destination should use a logon group defined in the target (transaction SMLG). It is common practice to create specific logon groups for RFC communication and to assign other groups for user logon. This way, the load created by RFC calls does not affect the performance for user activities.

Target resources

 We used function module RFC_SYSTEM_INFO for our first example. This module returns optional information on the current and maximum resources of the target system that we did not pay attention to before. The information even includes a recommended delay that should be considered before the next call. This suggests that the client application may consider handling target system resources. Nevertheless, as already mentioned, the **target** system must ensure adequate load balancing on its own and not rely on resource considerations on the client side.

The profile parameter auth/rfc_authority_check is essential for the authentication and authorization in the target system. The help documentation lists possible values for the parameter.

Help documentation for profile parameters

 To view the help documentation for profile parameters, start report RSPFPAR and specify the relevant parameter (e.g. *auth/rfc_authority_check*). Execute the report by pressing [F8], choose the respective line by pressing [F2], and then display the help documentation by pressing [F1].

The documentation reveals another aspect of why our first RFC example was cheating: for some values of rfc_authority_check, the execution of the function module RFC_SYSTEM_INFO does not require a user to log on. Check the function group SRFC that this module belongs to and you will find RFC_PING as another useful module for testing purposes.

Unified Connectivity (UCON)

The current concept of blocking remote access to function modules requires you to block each function separately. The concept of *Unified Connectivity* simplifies the control and allows access only to dedicated modules that have been registered. It was introduced with SAP_BASIS 7.40 and will be extended in the future.

1.4   Checking the remote enablement of modules

Now that we have our hand-made RFC destination, let's continue and do some investigation work. Our simplified RFC example executed a call to a function module without knowing whether the selected module can be executed remotely (using RFC).

In your report Z_RFC_IN_THREE_MINUTES, double-click the name of the function module RFC_SYSTEM_INFO to open it in the *Function Builder*. This *forward navigation* (inside the source system) works because the function module also exists in the source system.

Look at the ATTRIBUTES tab of the function module: in the PROCESSING TYPE area, the checkbox REMOTE-ENABLED MODULE is selected, as shown in Figure 1.5. This is the prerequisite for allowing the function module to be executed from within another system. We call these function modules *remote-enabled function modules (RFM)*.

Figure 1.5: Processing type "Remote-enabled module"

Note that the figure contains German text because the short text was not translated by SAP.

ABAP classes are not remote-enabled

ABAP classes do not offer this attribute as they cannot be executed from outside the system using RFC. Later, we will discuss whether protocols other than RFC allow this.

We have investigated the attributes of the function module in the **source** system—of course, it is relevant that the function module is remote-enabled in the **target** system. It is not a requirement for an RFC that the function module called exists in the source system as well.

Nevertheless, it is helpful if the module exists in the source system and not only for using forward navigation; if the module does exist in the source system, this allows you to use the PATTERN feature of the editor to create the CALL FUNCTION skeleton and to then add the destination manually. But of course, this presumes that the interfaces of local and remote modules are identical.

Central repository for RFMs

This brings us to the question of whether there is a central interface repository for RFMs that an RFC client application can use for the syntax of the call. There is in fact no such global repository for function modules in a system landscape. The source of truth for the interface of a function module is always the target system.

Before executing an RFM from a client system, you should always test the RFM locally in the target system to familiarize yourself with its interface. Note that the test call is not a simulation, which means that the ABAP runtime will execute the ABAP coding without retention. The testing of modules is covered in *First Steps in ABAP* (Espresso Tutorials, 2013).

Start a test for the module from within the Function Builder—for example, by pressing the ⌨F8 function key. The initial screen of the test environment displays all parameters that the RFM may import based on the values in the IMPORTING and TABLES parts of the interface.

You will see that this specific function module RFC_SYSTEM_INFO does not require any input as it has no parameters in the IMPORTING or TABLES sections. However, it does have a text field RFC TARGET SYS, as shown in Figure 1.6. You can use this field to enter the name of your RFC destination.

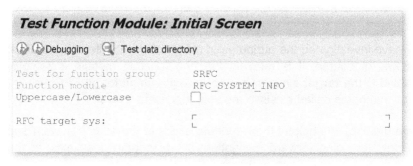

Figure 1.6: Initial screen of the test environment with field "RFC target sys"

The Function Builder offers this field only for remote-enabled function modules and it assumes that an identical function module exists in the target system. By entering a valid destination in this field, you turn the local test call into an RFC.

Therefore, the test environment of the Function Builder offers a simple RFC test function. However, the function is limited: it only works if the function module exists on both the client and server sides and if the interface is identical on both sides.

You can execute the test from the source system as well to get the results that you already know from your report (see Figure 1.7) by opening the structure *RFCSI_EXPORT* (click on the icon next to the number under VALUE).

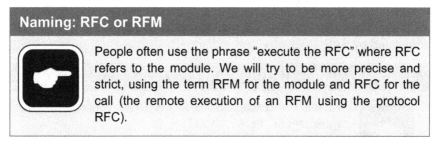

Test Function Module: Result Screen

Test for function group   SRFC
Function module   RFC_SYSTEM_INFO
Uppercase/Lowercase   ☐

Runtime: 298.203 Microseconds

RFC target sys: FIRSTDEST

Export parameters	Value
RFCSI_EXPORT	🗒 0114103LITIE3wdfl
CURRENT_RESOURCES	22
MAXIMAL_RESOURCES	24
RECOMMENDED_DELAY	0

Figure 1.7: Result screen for testing RFC_SYSTEM_INFO

Let us now focus on something else, related to the runtime shown on the result screen. This parameter indicates the duration of the call (request, logon, and response). Keep the current value in mind, go back to the initial screen by pressing F3, and execute another test—the value is much smaller now. This is because the connection to the target system is kept open as long as the RFC client application is live. In our case, the client application is the test environment. If you leave the test environment of the Function Builder and then return to it for the next test, the runtime will be higher again.

Naming: RFC or RFM

People often use the phrase "execute the RFC" where RFC refers to the module. We will try to be more precise and strict, using the term RFM for the module and RFC for the call (the remote execution of an RFM using the protocol RFC).

The RFM RFC_SYSTEM_INFO that we have used so far is of course too simple; it has no parameters in the IMPORTING and TABLES sections and no exceptions. Let's discuss exceptions now.

1.5 Handling RFC exceptions

The RFM itself may have exceptions as part of the interface—these are listed on the EXCEPTIONS tab (see Figure 1.8). The coding of the module foresees error situations and notifies the client of such situations via an exception. Examples include the RFC call not having mandatory parameters, or the call providing invalid values. Of course, exceptions defined in the RFM do not cover issues outside the RFM, such as connectivity problems.

A client application must consider the defined exceptions in the interface part of the RFC call statement, in the section EXCEPTIONS.

Let's use the RFM DEMO_RFM_CLASSIC_EXCEPTION as a simple example. The RFM has no implementation logic apart from raising the exception CLASSIC_EXCEPTION (using the RAISING statement).

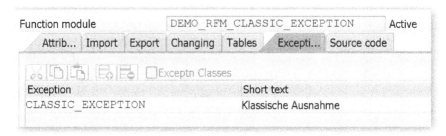

Figure 1.8: Exceptions section of a function module

Note that the figure contains German text because the short text was not translated by SAP.

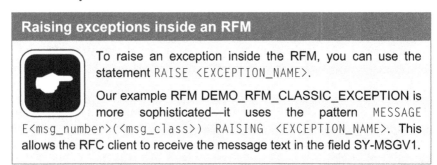

Raising exceptions inside an RFM

To raise an exception inside the RFM, you can use the statement RAISE <EXCEPTION_NAME>.

Our example RFM DEMO_RFM_CLASSIC_EXCEPTION is more sophisticated—it uses the pattern MESSAGE E<msg_number>(<msg_class>) RAISING <EXCEPTION_NAME>. This allows the RFC client to receive the message text in the field SY-MSGV1.

Any RFC client application that calls this RFM must handle this exception. The exception is assigned to a number—if the exception occurs, the value in the field SY-SUBRC equals this number.

In addition, two generic RFC exceptions provided by the RFC runtime should be caught:

▶ SYSTEM_FAILURE is raised if an issue occurs in the target system (e.g., the RFM does not exist)

▶ COMMUNICATION_FAILURE is raised in the case of communication issues (e.g., the RFC destination does not exist)

This leads to the example report Z_RFM_EXCPTN (see Listing 1.3).

```
REPORT Z_RFM_EXCEPTN.

Parameters: pa_dest
    type RFCDES-RFCDEST default 'FIRSTDEST'.

Data: gv_msg(100).

CALL FUNCTION 'DEMO_RFM_CLASSIC_EXCEPTION'
  destination pa_dest
  EXCEPTIONS
    CLASSIC_EXCEPTION     = 1
    SYSTEM_FAILURE        = 2 MESSAGE gv_msg
    COMMUNICATION_FAILURE = 3 MESSAGE gv_msg.

CASE sy-subrc.
  WHEN 1.
    WRITE: sy-subrc, sy-msgv1.
  WHEN 2.
    WRITE: sy-subrc, gv_msg.
  WHEN 3.
    WRITE: sy-subrc, gv_msg.
ENDCASE.
```

Listing 1.3: Report for catching exceptions

The RFC-specific exceptions offer additional text which can be put into a variable with the addition `MESSAGE`. This addition is not available for the exceptions defined in the RFM.

Triggering different exceptions

▶ Run the report with a valid RFC destination to check that `CLASSIC_EXCEPTION` is raised by the RFM and caught by the report.

▶ Run the report again and use an invalid name for the RFC destination to check that `COMMUNICATION_FAILURE` is caught.

▶ Now modify the report to call an RFM that does not exist (e.g., DEMO_RFM_CLASSIC_ EXCEPTION_2) to check that `SYSTEM_FAILURE` is caught.

In general, function modules may use *class-based exceptions* instead of the classical exceptions. You can see this on the EXCEPTIONS tab in the properties of the function module, as shown in Figure 1.9. The checkbox EXCEPTN CLASSES is selected for the function module DEMO_RFM_CLASS_BASED_EXCEPTION.

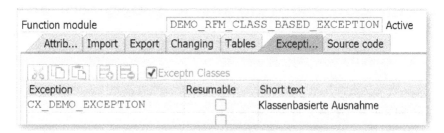

Figure 1.9: Class-based exceptions: not applicable for RFC

Note that the figure contains German text because the short text was not translated by SAP. For the local execution of the function module, such a class-based exception requires the calling application to use the `TRY/CATCH` block. For an RFC, however, the `TRY/CATCH` block is not required, as such exceptions are handled as `SYSTEM_FAILURE` exceptions.

Class-based exceptions for RFC

 There was an intermediate release phase in which class-based exceptions required a TRY/CATCH block for RFC as well. These releases were based on SAP_BASIS 7.20 and 7.30. However, these component versions were never used for any ABAP system that is part of the SAP Business Suite (e.g., SAP ECC). Since 7.40, the class-based exceptions are handled via the exception SYSTEM_FAILURE for RFC.

Let's put this into another example: Listing 1.4 shows report Z_RFM_CB _EXC.

```
REPORT Z_RFM_CB_EXC.

PARAMETERS: pa_dest TYPE rfcdes-rfcdest DEFAULT 'FIRSTDEST'.

DATA: gv_msg(100),
      exc TYPE REF TO cx_demo_exception.

TRY.
    CALL FUNCTION 'DEMO_RFM_CLASS_BASED_EXCEPTION'
      DESTINATION pa_dest
      EXCEPTIONS
        system_failure        = 1  MESSAGE gv_msg
        communication_failure = 2  MESSAGE gv_msg.
    WRITE: 'SY-SUBRC: ', sy-subrc, gv_msg.
  CATCH cx_demo_exception INTO exc.
    gv_msg = exc->get_text( ) .
    WRITE: 'catch block: ',  gv_msg.
ENDTRY.
```

Listing 1.4: Report catching class-based exceptions

Method get_text

Note that the respective SAP release determines whether the syntax check allows the result of method `get_text` to be written directly or whether a variable has to be used, like gv_msg in Listing 1.4.

```
CATCH cx_demo_exception INTO exc.
   WRITE: exc->get_text( ) .
```

The line above does not work for all releases.

The coding block above nevertheless encapsulates the `CALL FUNCTION` statement in a `TRY/CATCH` block. This is required if you initiate a local call using a destination with content `SPACE`: for this type of local call, the exception `SYSTEM_FAILURE` is not valid and the class-based exception has to be caught instead.

Catching class-based exceptions

Execute the report to check that the class-based RFM exception is handled with `SYSTEM_FAILURE`. You can provoke the `COMMUNICATION_FAILURE` exception again by providing the name of a destination that does not exist. Executing the report with destination `SPACE` (set `pa_dest` to empty!) triggers a local call of the module and thus ends in the `CATCH` block.

Exceptions defined in the interface of the RFM have the advantage that the RFM can let us know about the reason for an error. Sometimes you want to investigate the details of what happens inside the function module, therefore it is useful to know about remote debugging of RFMs. We will take a look at this aspect now.

1.6 Remote debugging of RFMs

Remote debugging of RFMs means debugging the code of the remote function module from within the source system. This allows you to investigate how the data provided is received inside the module.

The prerequisites for remote debugging are as follows:

▶ The logon must use a dialog user (either specified in the RFC destination or provided on the logon screen)

▶ The user requires all necessary authorizations (especially for debugging, and for all statements that the RFM executes)

▶ The target system is an ABAP system

You can set an external breakpoint inside the function module (in the target system!) to start the debugger, as illustrated in Figure 1.10.

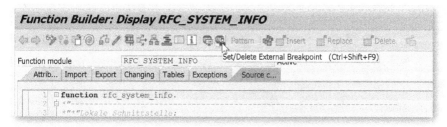

Figure 1.10: Setting an external breakpoint inside an RFM

Note that the figure contains German text because text that was not translated by SAP was inserted automatically.

These external breakpoints are user-specific, so the user for which the breakpoint was set has to be used to log on to this target system for the breakpoint to work.

However, you can also simply debug your client application: set a breakpoint for the RFC statement and step into the statement to jump into the coding of the (target) function module.

When debugging the function module, you can check the variable SY-SYSID to verify that you are working on the target system.

Now imagine the case in which the RFM is used as the target for several client applications which may even be executed in different client systems. If all the RFC destinations in the client systems use the same user to log on, the external breakpoint for this user would impact all client applications. This is certainly not desirable, as you want the debugger to be used only for your client application session and not for all sessions.

The concept of the *terminal ID* was introduced to overcome this situation. It allows you to set a breakpoint which is specific for a dedicated client only. The client is identified by a client-specific ID—the terminal ID—for which the breakpoint is set. Debugging only happens, therefore, if the request is sent from this specific client.

The settings allow you to switch from **user-related** to **terminal ID-related** external breakpoints. Select UTILITIES/SETTINGS • ABAP EDITOR • DEBUGGING • DEBUGGING EXTERNAL REQUESTS to select TERMINAL ID instead of USER. A terminal ID is generated for the PC on which the SAPGUI is running and is shown in the dialog box, as illustrated in Figure 1.11.

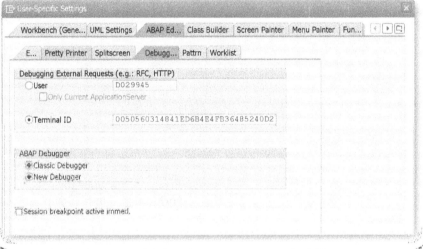

Figure 1.11: Setting external debugging requests to terminal ID

If you set an external breakpoint after this adjustment, the related success message (on the lower part of the SAP GUI screen) shows that the breakpoint is related to the terminal ID.

But how do you provide this terminal ID from your client application? It's quite simple: you use the command */hset tid=<tid>* in the command field to set the terminal ID before starting the client application (<tid> is the terminal ID for which the debugging was activated).

If you start your client application from the same PC on which you have switched to terminal ID debugging (Figure 1.11), you use only */htid*. This works for Windows PCs only.

Using these commands ensures that the terminal ID is provided to the target server and the debugging is enabled.

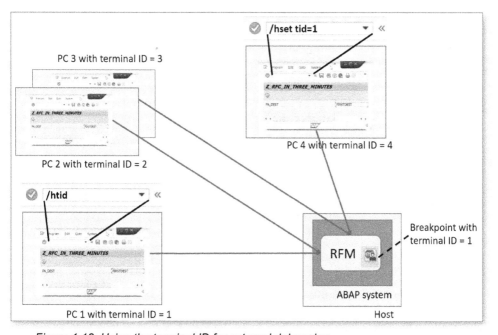

Figure 1.12: Using the terminal ID for external debugging

Figure 1.12 illustrates the approach: for the sake of simplicity, we assume a terminal ID of one digit and use this number for the PC as well.

We switch on the external debugging using the terminal ID while working on PC 1 and we set a breakpoint in the RFM. Executing our report from PC 1 does not start the debugging; it only starts if we use the command */htid*. Executing our report from other PCs will also not start the debugging unless we use the command */hset tid=1*, as shown for PC 4.

Remote debugging allows you to check what happens inside the RFM in the target system. However, if your call does not reach the target, you may want to investigate the wire and traces. In this case, the gateway is the place to start.

1.7   Monitoring connections on the gateway

The *gateway* is a process that runs on the ABAP host. It is the relay station for the RFC communication and offers the *Gateway Monitor* for checking existing communication. Each *ABAP instance* (also referred to as the *application server* from a software perspective) consists of several work processes and one *gateway service*, the executable that represents the gateway.

SAP Gateway versus gateway

The gateway as part of an instance is an executable. Although it sounds similar, the *SAP Gateway* is something else—an SAP product that enables ABAP systems for communication using OData.

Start your report Z_RFC_IN_THREE_MINUTES and keep the result (list) open, thereby keeping the application live. This keeps the RFC connection open, as discussed in Section 1.4. Open the Gateway Monitor with transaction SMGW in a separate session: it will show one line in the table with your connection (see Figure 1.13).

Gateway Monitor for wdflbmd15859.wdf.sap.corp / Active Connections

Numb	Longer LU name	Longer TP name	Remote LU name	Remote TP name	Users	Status	Destination	ConvID	
6	wdflbmd15859.w	sapgw00	10.76.195.236	sapdp00	D029945	Connected	FIRSTDES	90588749	I

Figure 1.13: Gateway Monitor (transaction SMGW) shows active connections

This illustrates that the connection between client and server is maintained as long as the client context exists (that is: the client application is still running).

But the explanation above was not accurate: it did not tell you which system to open the Gateway Monitor in! The RFC is handled on a target application server on which the RFM is executed. Therefore, the respective gateway of this target **instance** will also be involved, just like the gateway of the client instance. Both Gateway Monitors display the connection (see Figure 1.14).

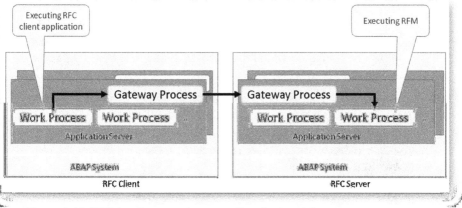

Figure 1.14: RFC involves a gateway on the client and the server

Therefore, remember to use both Gateway Monitors if you are having connectivity issues to ensure that the call reaches your desired target system and no other system.

Checking the target gateway if the scenario does not work

When you maintain an RFC destination in transaction SM59, you have access to an easy connection test to check whether the target system can be reached.

Imagine the case in which the RFC destination unintentionally points to a different system in which the password is not valid. The connection test works but your scenario does not: you get incorrect data. In the worst case, the use of such a destination may lock the user in the target system due to too many failed logon attempts. Checking the Gateway Monitor in the target system can reveal whether the destination points to the correct system.

A real live system typically runs on several instances, as suggested in Figure 1.14. On which instance of the RFC server system do you have to check the Gateway Monitor? It depends on whether one specific gateway has been maintained in the RFC destination (in the RFC client system).

Gateway specification in the RFC destination

 If you did not maintain one specific gateway in the RFC destination, the source system uses the gateway of the instance on which the client application is being processed (in a work process).

To assign a different gateway in the RFC destination, use the GATEWAY OPTIONS area (tab TECHNICAL SETTINGS). Enter the IP name (or address) of the instance in the GATEWAY HOST field and *sagpw<nr>* (where <nr> is the respective instance number) in the GATEWAY SERVICE field.

In addition to checking existing connections, you can also use the Gateway Monitor to check traces, so let's focus on this aspect now.

1.8 Checking RFC traces

The Gateway Monitor is not the only location for traces. You can use the following traces:

▶ Gateway trace

You can check the trace in the Gateway Monitor (transaction SMGW) by selecting GOTO • TRACE • GATEWAY • DISPLAY TRACEFILE. You can adapt the trace level by selecting GOTO • TRACE • GATEWAY • INCREASE LEVEL (or DECREASE respectively). You can only see the result and the current trace level in the trace itself, with a line such as `* SWITCH TRC-LEVEL from 1 TO 2`.

The trace contains information such as the data transferred, the destination name, and the user (see Figure 1.15)—but not the password, of course.

Gateway monitor for wdflbmd15859.wdf.sap.corp / trace file

```
000000000FAA3D60  000400  20001300 12000437 34302000 12000600  | ......740 .....
000000000FAA3D70  000416  09464952 53544445 53540006 01300016  |.FIRSTDEST...O..
000000000FAA3D80  000432  5a5f5246 435f494e 5f544852 45455f4d  |Z_RFC_IN_THREE_M
000000000FAA3D90  000448  494e5554 45530130 01110007 44303239  |INUTES.O....D029
000000000FAA3DA0  000464  39343501 11011700 0a88a8b4 9f3b071e  |945..........;..
000000000FAA3DB0  000480  32467701 17000300 03444d53 0003000c  |2Fw......DMS....
```

Figure 1.15: Example of a gateway trace

▶ Destination trace

In an RFC destination, use the SPECIAL OPTIONS tab to enable the RFC trace for a destination. You can check the traces for RFC destinations by choosing RFC • DISPLAY TRACE in the list of destinations (transaction SM59). This lists separated traces (e.g., dev_rfc*) and shows the content similar to the gateway trace above.

▶ ST05 trace

You can activate and check the RFC trace in the *performance analysis* (transaction ST05).

Traces have an impact on performance

Do not forget to subsequently deactivate these traces because they have a negative impact on the server performance.

Trace or log?

You use *logs* for error reporting; they are provided when errors occur. If you want to follow your program flow and data, switch on *traces* temporarily for the time of your analysis. For RFC, there are no specific log files apart from the RFM exceptions and runtime errors shown in transaction ST22.

Up to this point, we already had the names of the RFMs to be called, which is not a real-life situation. Let's discuss how to search for an RFM that fulfills the requirements of your project.

1.9   Searching for RFMs

You search for RFMs on the initial screen of the Function Builder or using the *Repository Information System* (transaction SE84)—both lead to the same dialog. Starting in the Function Builder, use the F4 help to open the search dialog, as depicted by the icon circled in the upper part of Figure 1.16.

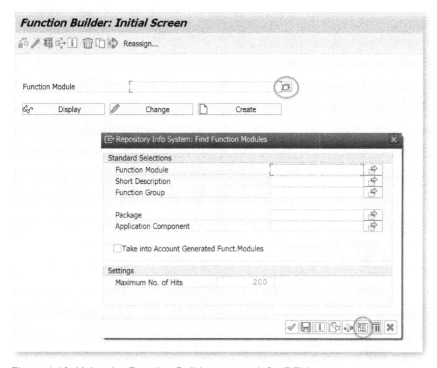

Figure 1.16: Using the Function Builder to search for RFMs

On the search screen, click ALL SELECTIONS ⟨⇧⟩ + F7 (circled in the lower part of Figure 1.16) to expand the search options with additional selections. This is the only way to narrow the search for the remote-enabled attribute (checkbox RFC MODULES) (see Figure 1.17).

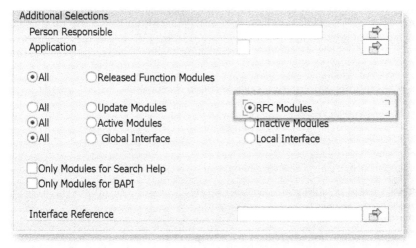

Figure 1.17: Additional selections when searching for RFMs

The search considers only the local repository, so it is a local search in the system in which you have logged on. Therefore, you should do the search in the target system in which you want to execute the RFM. Keep in mind that there is no global repository of the RFMs of all systems in the landscape.

If your search does not find an RFM that fits your scenario, you may want to consider creating your own interface.

1.10 Creating your own data objects

Before we work on our own interface example, we must first create some objects at database and application level—in the target system.

Although learning about interface technologies sometimes seems like completing a marathon, it is worthwhile. The scenario for our custom objects is rather sporty as well: it is based on data for athletes. This data will be stored in a central system and will be accessible for external applications via RFC.

We will create the following objects as the foundation for the interfaces which we will create afterwards:

▶ Database table

▶ Authorization object, authorization, and role

▶ Message class

▶ Lock objects

▶ Number range

We will create a table with basic information about the athlete (ID, name, date of birth, country).

Custom package ZSPORTS

You can create your own package for all your objects so that you can transport the objects later. We will use package ZSPORTS with a leading Z for the customer namespace.

Therefore, we create database table ZATHLETE as part of the package ZSPORTS. Create the table, maintain a short text, and maintain the delivery class as *A*. Set the parameter DATA BROWSER/TABLE VIEW MAINT. to *Display/Maintenance allowed*.

Then maintain the respective fields as shown in Figure 1.18.

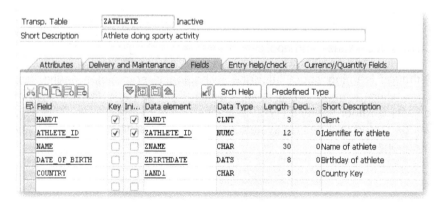

| Transp. Table | ZATHLETE | Inactive |
| Short Description | Athlete doing sporty activity | |

Field	Key	Ini...	Data element	Data Type	Length	Deci...	Short Description
MANDT	✓	✓	MANDT	CLNT	3	0	Client
ATHLETE_ID	✓	✓	ZATHLETE_ID	NUMC	12	0	Identifier for athlete
NAME	☐	☐	ZNAME	CHAR	30	0	Name of athlete
DATE_OF_BIRTH	☐	☐	ZBIRTHDATE	DATS	8	0	Birthday of athlete
COUNTRY	☐	☐	LAND1	CHAR	3	0	Country Key
	☐	☐					

Figure 1.18: New transparent table ZATHLETE

Create and reference your own data elements, as shown in Figure 1.18.

For the field *COUNTRY*, specify a foreign key: select the line, then select the icon 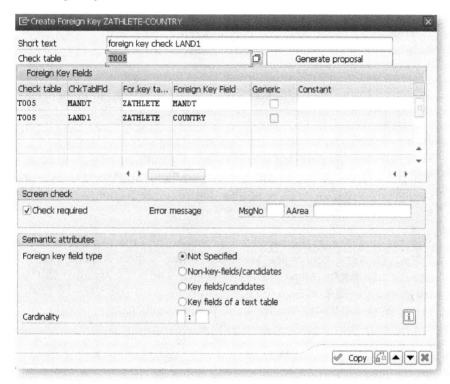 FOREIGN KEYS. Confirm the dialog box to create a proposal with values table T005. In the subsequent dialog box (see Figure 1.19), enter a short text and click COPY to close the dialog box and to transfer the foreign key.

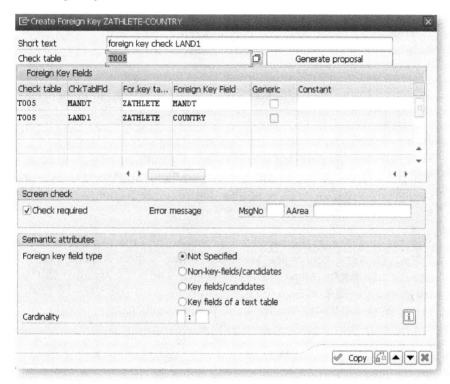

Figure 1.19: Creating a foreign key for the field COUNTRY

Save the table. Choose GOTO • TECHNICAL SETTINGS to set DATA CLASS to *APPL0* and SIZE CATEGORY to *0*. Choose EXTRAS • ENHANCEMENT CATE-GORIES to set enhancement categories to *Can Be Enhanced (Deep)*. Finally, activate the table.

It is a good idea to enter information in the table so that our RFMs can provide data later. In the table maintenance function, choose UTILITIES • TABLE CONTENTS • CREATE ENTRIES and create several entries for the table.

Prerequisite for direct table maintenance

 There are two prerequisites for allowing direct maintenance of table entries from transaction SE11. The first
prerequisite is that we have already prepared the table-
specific part on the DELIVERY AND MAINTENANCE tab in the
TABLE VIEW MAINT. area, as described above. Secondly,
the client settings must allow the maintenance, which is typically not
the case for client 000. You can check the client-specific settings in
transaction SCC4.

To restrict the access to our athletic results, we create an authorization
object. Use the context menu on our package ZSPORTS and select
CREATE • OTHER (1) • AUTHORIZATION OBJECT. Specify *ZATHLETE* in the
OBJECT field, enter a text in the TEXT field, and enter the value *BC_A* in
the CLASS field (see the left part of Figure 1.20). Press ⌷Enter⌷ to enable
the AUTHORIZATION FIELDS table, enter the field *ACTVT*, and click the
column SHORT DESCRIPTION so that the respective information for the
existing field is provided. Save the object.

You can now assign the permitted activities using the respective button
PERMITTED ACTIVITIES on the lower part of the screen. A dialog box DE-
FINE VALUES opens. Allow the values *01* (Create), *02* (Change), *03* (Dis-
play), and *06* (Delete) (see the right part of Figure 1.20). Click 🔲 TRANS-
FER to close the dialog box and close the new authorization object.

In the next step, we have to create an *authorization* for the authorization
object and assign this authorization to our user. Start the *Profile Genera-
tor* (transaction PFCG), enter the role name *ZATHLETE*, and click SIN-
GLE ROLE to create the role. You have to maintain a short text and save
the role before you can continue. Choose the AUTHORIZATIONS tab—this
is displayed with a red icon because no profile is maintained and no authorization data exists (see Figure 1.21).

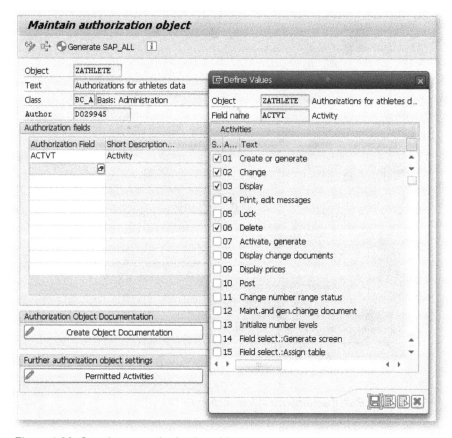

Figure 1.20: Creating an authorization object

On the AUTHORIZATIONS tab, click ✐ CHANGE AUTHORIZATION DATA. The first dialog box lists information for first-time users, the second dialog box offers templates. Close the latter by clicking ❌ Do not select templates . Now the screen for maintaining role authorizations is displayed (see Figure 1.22).

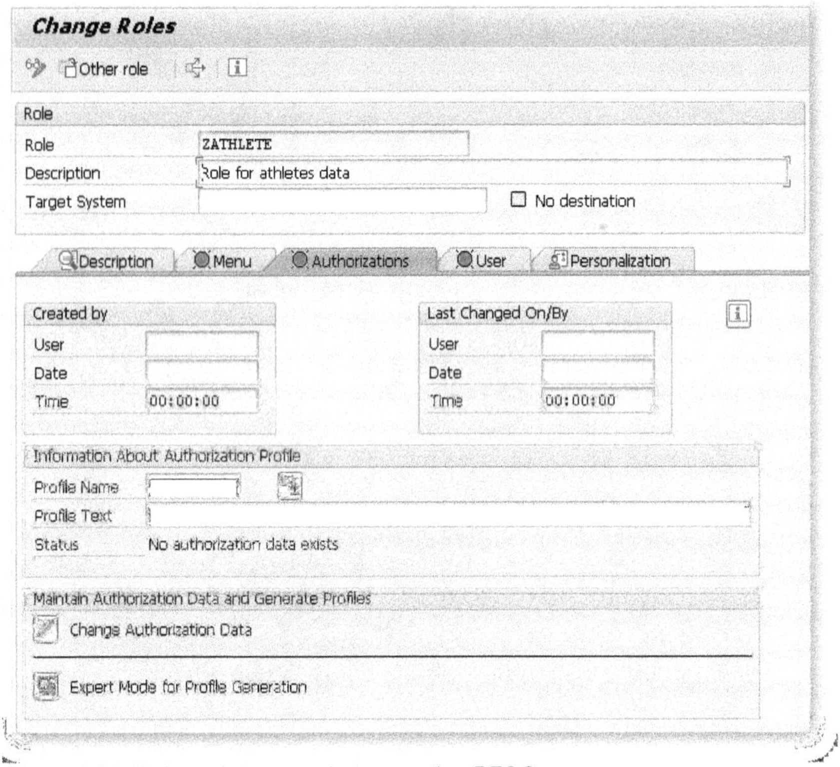

Figure 1.21: Role maintenance in transaction PFCG

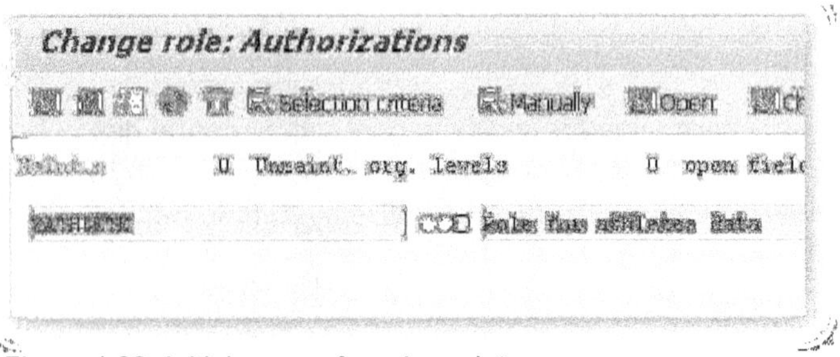

Figure 1.22: Initial screen for role maintenance

Click 🔲 Manually, add the authorization object *ZATHLETE* in the dialog box, and close the dialog box. Now we have to maintain the activities, so open the complete hierarchy down to the line ACTIVITY as shown in Figure 1.23.

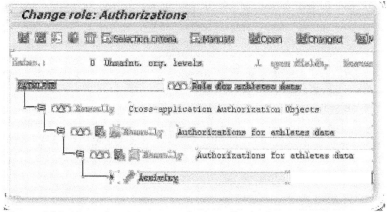

Figure 1.23: Manual maintenance of role authorization

By clicking the yellow icon ∗ (EMPTY FIELD), we can easily assign all activities—the yellow icons turn green. Save the role and accept the proposed name for the profile. Use the icon ⊕ to generate the role and press ⌊F3⌋ to navigate back to the role overview. The profile name is added and the AUTHORIZATIONS tab is now displayed with a green icon.

Choose the USER tab to maintain your user ID in the USER ASSIGNMENTS table (left part of Figure 1.24). Save the role, then click USER COMPARISON and click COMPLETE COMPARISON in the dialog box to have the authorization assigned to your user (right part of Figure 1.24).

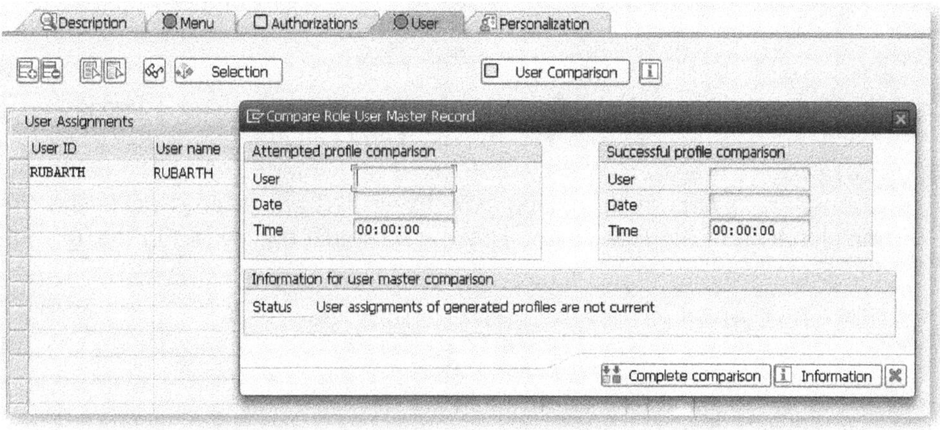

Figure 1.24: User assignment to a role

The successful profile comparison is listed in the upper right-hand side of the dialog box (fields USER, DATE, and TIME). Close the dialog box by clicking 🗙.

The USER tab now appears with a green icon as well. The role assignment to your user prepares your user for the AUTHORITY-CHECK statement that we will implement in the coding later. Save the role. Back in the Object Navigator, create a *message class* for the package ZSPORTS, using the context menu CREATE • OTHER (1) • MESSAGE CLASS. Enter the name *ZSPORTS* and enter the following messages:

```
000    & & & &
001    Error during processing: &
002    Missing authorization
003    Invalid data
004    No entry found
005    Object locked
```

Table 1.1: Messages for message class ZSPORTS

Objects for database changes

 The following two objects (lock object and number range) will only be relevant later when we extend our data model to function modules writing data to the database.

We have to create a lock object to follow the principle of the ABAP lock mechanism. Therefore, use the context menu CREATE • DICTIONARY OBJECT • LOCK OBJECT on package ZSPORTS and enter *EZATHLETE* in the LOCK OBJECT field in the dialog box. Press [Enter] to proceed to the maintenance of the lock object. Enter a short text and switch to the TABLES tab (see Figure 1.25).

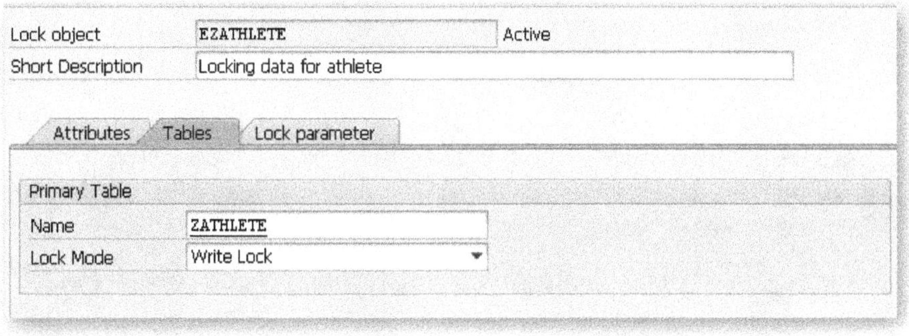

Lock object	EZATHLETE	Active
Short Description	Locking data for athlete	

Attributes	Tables	Lock parameter

Primary Table

Name	ZATHLETE
Lock Mode	Write Lock ▾

Figure 1.25: Lock object maintenance

Specify table *ZATHLETE* as the primary table on the TABLES tab, specifying the value *Write Lock* for the LOCK MODE field. Activate the object and choose GOTO • LOCK MODULES to verify that the function modules ENQUEUE_ZATHLETE and DEQUEUE_ZATHLETE were created.

To enable continuous numbering of our athletes, we need an internal number range. Start transaction SNRO, enter ZATHLETE as the object name and click 📷 to create the number range object. Specify a short and long text for the object. Set the NUMBER LENGTH DOMAIN field to *CHAR10* and the WARNING % field to *10.0* (see Figure 1.26). Save the object and confirm the warning in the dialog box with YES.

Now click NUMBER RANGES and then ⟨ Intervals ⟩ CHANGE INTERVALS to display the list of intervals. Click the 📇 icon, and in the dialog box, enter a new interval *1* ranging from *0000000001* to *0000010000* (see Figure 1.27).

Press [Enter] to close the dialog box, save the number range, and ignore the warning that appears.

Number Range Object: Change

Change Documents | Number Ranges |

| Object | ZATHLETE | Number range object has no intervals |

Short text   ZATHLETE

Long text   ZATHLETE

Interval characteristics

Subobject data element

To-year flag   ☐

Number length domain   CHAR10

No interval rolling   ☐

Customizing specifications

Number range transaction

Warning %   10,0

Main memory buffering   ☑   No. of numbers in buffer   10

Group specification

Figure 1.26: Create number range object

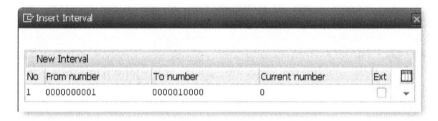

Insert Interval

New Interval

No	From number	To number	Current number	Ext	
1	0000000001	0000010000	0	☐	▼

Figure 1.27: Inserting a new interval for a number range

The object list for our package now shows the ABAP objects, see Figure 1.28. The number range, the role, and the authorization are not listed here.

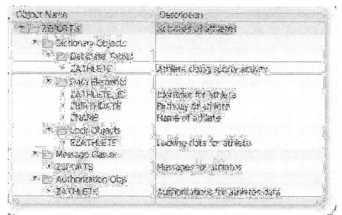

Figure 1.28: Object list of our own objects as preparation

1.11 Creating RFMs to read data

We will now create a new RFM in the *Object Navigator* to provide details about a specific athlete.

Our module will have to import the athlete ID and will export the details such as name, date of birth, and country.

The sequence of steps for creating an RFM is as follows:

0) Create a function group

1) Create the function module, set it to REMOTE-ENABLED

2) Maintain the interface sections

3) Implement the coding

4) Test your function module locally

5) Use your function module remotely via RFC

Objects in the target system

 Hopefully, you have two distinct systems available for your development and not just two different clients in one system. Using two different systems will illustrate that for custom development in particular, the RFM interface is typically only available in the target system. Therefore, we will create all objects (steps 0 to 4) in the target system in which we created the foundation objects (Section 1.10).

0) Create a *function group*

Function modules are always bundled in a function group, so first we have to create the group. However, in the case of several modules belonging to the same application context, you will use just one group. This is why the step is numbered 0, as it is not always required.

Use the context menu CREATE • FUNCTION GROUP and enter the name *ZSPORTS* for the function group. Add a short text, keep your user as PERSON RESPONSIBLE, and press [Enter] to create the function group. Note that the name of the group is not relevant in any way for external communication.

The TOP include of the function group may be used for global definitions that can be used in each function module of the group.

1) Create the function module

Create the RFM as part of the function group and call it Z_ATHLETE_ READ_DETAILS.

Prefix Z_ for custom function modules

 If you try to create the function module with the prefix ZATHLETE_ (no underscore after the Z), the workbench will display an information box stating that the module name is reserved for SAP. Although you can ignore this message, we recommend that you use Z_ as the prefix, as proposed above: Z_ATHLETE_.

Note that you can even use a name without the prefix Z at all (but this is not recommended either) because internally, the modules are stored as includes.

Switch to the ATTRIBUTES tab and in the PROCESSING TYPE area, select REMOTE-ENABLED MODULE.

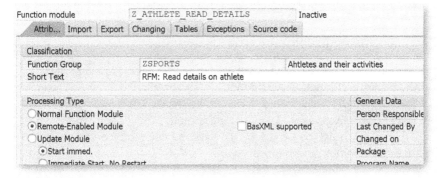

Figure 1.29: Function module attributes for remote enablement

As shown in Figure 1.29 above, we have included the prefix *RFM* in the short text of the module. This is not required but may be helpful later, when the function group contains other module types as well.

2) Maintain the interface sections

Start by maintaining the parameters on the IMPORT tab.

It is common practice to use a prefix I_ (upper case i) for import parameters and E_ for export parameters. This corresponds to the SAP naming guidelines (referenced at the end of Section 1.1). Figure 1.30 shows the import section of our module.

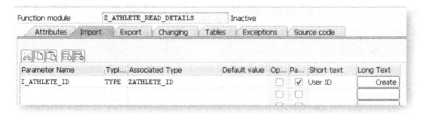

Figure 1.30: Import section of RFM Z_ATHLETE_READ_DETAILS

Interface requirements for remote-enabled modules

 You will experience the consequences of having selected REMOTE-ENABLED MODULE for the module interface design. All parameters have to be typed, referencing the Data Dictionary (DDIC). Furthermore, the option PASS VALUE must be selected, as pass by reference does not make sense for a remote communication.

Finish the interface sections with the parameters that are listed under Local Interface in the following coding block (Listing 1.5).

```
*"*"Local Interface:
*"  IMPORTING
*"     VALUE(I_ATHLETE_ID) TYPE  ZATHLETE_ID
*"  EXPORTING
*"     VALUE(E_NAME) TYPE ZNAME
*"     VALUE(E_DATE_OF_BIRTH) TYPE  ZBIRTHDATE
*"     VALUE(E_COUNTRY) TYPE  LAND1
*"  EXCEPTIONS
*"     ATHLETE_NOT_FOUND
```

```
*"      INVALID_DATA
*"      MISSING_AUTHORIZATION
```

Listing 1.5: Interface of RFM Z_ATHLETE_READ_DETAILS

RFM interface considerations

 Structures listed on the TABLES tab are simultaneously import and export parameters. Both directions are not used in all cases; the direction that is relevant depends on the actual function module.

Meanwhile, you can also use the CHANGING tab for RFC, although this is typically still not used. The restriction to not use changing parameters is no longer valid in SAP_BASIS 7.0 and above. You can even use table structures in the IMPORTING and EXPORTING sections.

Note that the RFC protocol has the advantage of transferring only the delta in the response for the structures defined in the TABLES section. Depending on the scenario, this can be a big performance advantage.

3) Implement the coding

Cover the usual parts like the authority check, consistency checks, initialization of fields, and the respective SELECT statement on the database table. Listing 1.6 shows the respective coding proposal:

```
FUNCTION Z_ATHLETE_READ_DETAILS.

  DATA: ls_athlete TYPE zathlete.

* Authority check
  AUTHORITY-CHECK OBJECT 'ZATHLETE'
             ID 'ACTVT' FIELD '03'.
  IF sy-subrc NE 0.
    MESSAGE e002(zsports) RAISING missing_authorization.
  ENDIF.

* Consistency checks
  IF i_athlete_id IS INITIAL.
    MESSAGE e003(zsports) RAISING invalid_data.
```

```
ENDIF.

SELECT SINGLE * FROM zathlete INTO ls_athlete WHERE
   athlete_id = i_athlete_id.

IF sy-subrc NE 0.
   MESSAGE e004(zsports) RAISING athlete_not_found.
ENDIF.

e_name = ls_athlete-name.
e_date_of_birth = ls_athlete-date_of_birth.
e_country = ls_athlete-country.
ENDFUNCTION.
```

Listing 1.6: Coding block of RFM Z_ATHLETE_READ_DETAILS

In general, there are no technical restrictions for the coding of an RFM compared to a non-remote function module. However, you should avoid statements that create an ABAP dialog (e.g., CALL SCREEN or WRITE) otherwise the RFM can only be used from an ABAP source system and only with a dialog user. An external call from a non-ABAP client will fail, as the client will not be able to handle that *dynpro*.

RFM attributes

 Note that you will not find an attribute in the Function Builder for an RFM stating whether it creates a dialog or not (it uses, for example, the WRITE statement or dynpro technology).

Do not forget to document the RFM. You can do this for each interface parameter separately (click CREATE in the LONG TEXT column) as well as for the RFM overall (click FUNCTION MODULE DOCUMENTATION), as depicted in Figure 1.31.

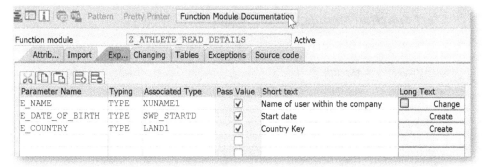

Figure 1.31: Documentation of the function module and parameters

After checking and activating the RFM, you can test it locally in the target system.

4) Test the function module

Start the test environment by pressing ⌐F8⌐ from within the display of the function module. Again, you will see the RFC TARGET SYS field. However, as this brand new (and customer-specific) RFM exists only in the local system and not in any remote system, the field is of no use to us. You would only benefit from this if your client and server systems were separate clients in the same system and thus shared the same data directory.

Execute the test with various values to check that the module works as expected. In particular, this will reveal whether you have already entered data in the database table.

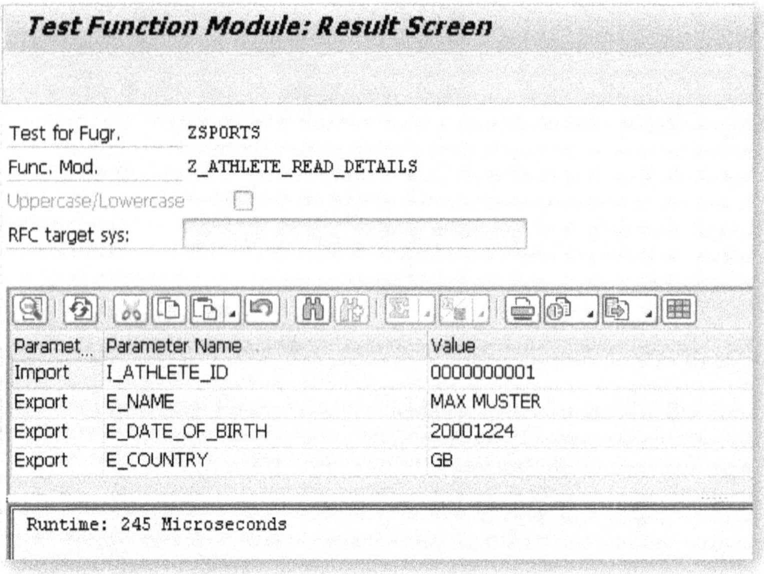

Test Function Module: Result Screen

Test for Fugr.   ZSPORTS

Func. Mod.   Z_ATHLETE_READ_DETAILS

Uppercase/Lowercase   ☐

RFC target sys:

Paramet...	Parameter Name	Value
Import	I_ATHLETE_ID	0000000001
Export	E_NAME	MAX MUSTER
Export	E_DATE_OF_BIRTH	20001224
Export	E_COUNTRY	GB

Runtime: 245 Microseconds

Figure 1.32: Test result screen for Z_ATHLETE_READ_DETAILS

Figure 1.32 should hold two surprises for you: the design of the list and the format of the date. Both are dependent on user-specific settings for testing, so let us take a moment to discuss these.

Navigate back to the display of the function module and open the workbench settings (UTILITIES • SETTINGS, FUNCTION BUILDER tab). The design of the test environment is determined by the ALV GRID DISPLAY FOR TEST ENVIRONMENT checkbox (see Figure 1.33), which allows use of the *ABAP List Viewer (ALV)*.

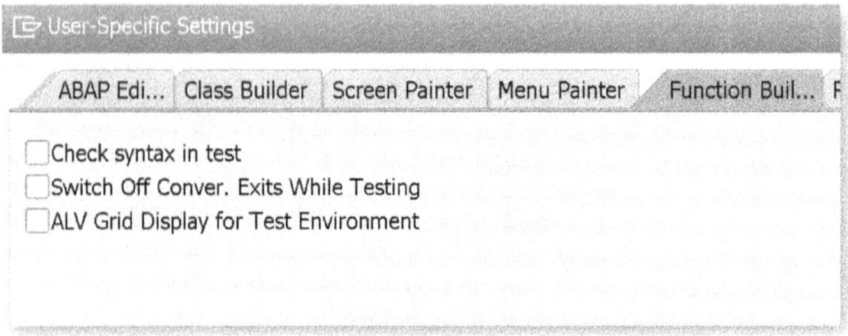

🗗 User-Specific Settings

| ABAP Edi... | Class Builder | Screen Painter | Menu Painter | Function Buil... | F |

☐ Check syntax in test
☐ Switch Off Conver. Exits While Testing
☐ ALV Grid Display for Test Environment

Figure 1.33: User-specific settings for the Function Builder

The SWITCH OFF CONVER. EXITS WHILE TESTING checkbox allows you to switch off *conversion exits*, which affects the display format for date and other fields.

User interface generated by the test environment

 The test environment provides the user interface (based on DynPro), which is not part of the RFM itself. For field types such as date, time, and others, this user interface may include conversion exits which convert the format of fields from internal ABAP format into the user-specific format.

For an RFC, the conversion exits will not be executed. For interface development, therefore, we recommend that you select the checkbox to switch off these conversions so that the test shows the same data format as the RFC would return to the client.

Common issue for testing

 This behavior of the Function Builder test environment is a common cause of confusion for parameters with conversion exits. Imagine that you successfully run a test using (user-specific) values for some parameters due to these conversion exits. This may mislead you to use the same value (user-specific format) in the RFC client application. However, as the RFC communication does not execute this conversion, the RFM will raise an error.

Checking the object list of your package, you may potentially detect an RFC SERVICES entry, as visible in Figure 1.34. Note that these object list entries are only relevant for the Unified Connectivity settings (see Section 1.3) and are shown only for some releases (for example, systems based on SAP_BASIS 7.40).

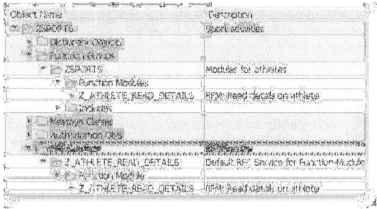

Figure 1.34: RFC services entry in the object list (7.40 only)

Just like for other ABAP objects, you can create a version for your RFM as well. Choose UTILITIES • VERSIONS to either create a version or to navigate to the version management of your RFM. Note that this is not identical to the versioning of an interface, as discussed later in Section 1.26.

You can also release your RFM by choosing FUNCTION MODULE • RELEASE • RELEASE. Note that for released modules, only compatible changes are allowed, such as adding optional parameters. If you try to make an incompatible change to a released module, the workbench will display a warning in a dialog box. Use the help icon in that dialog box to get additional information.

Do not use unreleased SAP function modules

 You must not use function modules that have not been released by SAP. These modules may be deleted by SAP without further notice, which may even happen as part of a Support Package applied to the system.

---

5) Execute your function module remotely via RFC

After we have created the RFC server functionality (the RFM), we can turn to the source system and create an RFC client application.

Function Builder test environment in the source system

 How about using the test environment of the Function Builder in the source system? Why don't we test the RFM remotely first before creating a client application?

That does not work because the source system is not aware of the RFM interface. The Function Builder in the source system cannot provide the test environment for the RFM. It has no access to the target system to retrieve the interface information. Remember that there is no central repository in ABAP for RFM interfaces.

Later, we will discuss the Extended Computer Aided Test Tool (e-CATT), which allows remote testing.

In this book, we create only simple reports and use parameters for data input, as we are focusing on interfaces and not on application development. Although the use of text variables is recommended, the coding examples use hard-coded text for WRITE statements so that you see the text in the example coding directly.

The coding of the client application checks whether the ID is filled and prevents the execution of the RFC if the parameter is initial. This way, no resources are occupied for a call that will return an error message anyway. Listing 1.7 shows the respective coding proposal for the RFC client application.

```
REPORT z_read_athlete_details.

PARAMETERS: pa_id(12) TYPE n,
pa_dest TYPE rfcdes-rfcdest DEFAULT 'FIRSTDEST'.

DATA: l_name(30), l_date TYPE dats, l_country TYPE LAND1,
 lv_msg(100).

IF pa_id IS INITIAL.
  WRITE: 'ID has to be provided'.
  EXIT.
  ENDIF.
```

```
CALL FUNCTION 'Z_ATHLETE_READ_DETAILS'
DESTINATION pa_dest
  EXPORTING
    i_athlete_id                = pa_id
  IMPORTING
    e_name                    = l_name
    e_date_of_birth           = l_date
    e_country                 = l_country

  EXCEPTIONS
    athlete_not_found         = 1
    invalid_data              = 2
    missing_authorization     = 3
    system_failure            = 4 MESSAGE lv_msg
    communication_failure     = 5 MESSAGE lv_msg
    OTHERS                    = 6
                      .
IF sy-subrc <> 0.
  WRITE: /, 'Remote response: ', sy-msgv1, lv_msg.
ELSE.
  WRITE: / l_name, l_date, l_country.
  ENDIF.
```

Listing 1.7: Report for an RFC to Z_ATHLETE_READ_DETAILS

As a kind of finger exercise, we will now implement the RFM Z_ATHLETES_LIST that provides a list of all existing athletes. Use a TABLES parameter to return the list of athletes. Clear the table variable at the beginning of your source code. This way, the code returns only the data from the database and omits data that may have been provided to the module via TABLES parameter.

As best practice, you should use an import parameter I_MAX_READ as a security measure, avoiding performance-intensive reads on large tables. Use the parameter as part of the SQL statement (UP TO i_max_read ROWS) to limit the number of table entries read from the database. Listing 1.8 shows the implementation proposal.

```
FUNCTION z_athletes_list.
*"----------------------------------------------------------
*"*"Local Interface:
*"  IMPORTING
*"     VALUE(I_MAX_READ) TYPE  INT4 DEFAULT 0
*"  TABLES
*"      T_ATHLETES STRUCTURE  ZATHLETE
*"  EXCEPTIONS
*"      ATHLETES_NOT_FOUND
*"      MISSING_AUTHORIZATION
*"----------------------------------------------------------
* Authority check
  AUTHORITY-CHECK OBJECT 'ZATHLETE'
          ID 'ACTVT' FIELD '03'.
  IF sy-subrc NE 0.
    MESSAGE e001(zsports) with 'missing authorization'
    RAISING missing_authorization.
  ENDIF.
  CLEAR t_athletes.
  SELECT * FROM zathlete INTO TABLE t_athletes
     UP TO i_max_read ROWS   .

  IF sy-subrc NE 0.
    MESSAGE e001(zsports) with 'no data'
    RAISING athletes_not_found.
  ENDIF.

ENDFUNCTION.
```

Listing 1.8: RFM Z_ATHLETES_LIST

We have now implemented the two basic operations for reading: either a list of all athletes or details for one athlete.

61

1.12 Extending code with an RFC statement

If you are not working on a new RFC client application and instead, want to extend existing code, you must consider that an RFC statement will trigger an *implicit COMMIT WORK*.

Therefore, putting an RFC statement between existing statements that belong to a *logical unit of work (LUW)* may potentially destroy this LUW.

Logical unit of work (LUW)

The logical unit of work (LUW) concept bundles together those database changes that have to be committed to the database together. If only part of the LUW is committed, the database is in an inconsistent state.

During the RFC statement on the client side, the work process rolls out the ABAP application context so that the work process can process other applications in the meantime. This improves the performance of the server as work processes are not occupied exclusively by one application. However, it also leads to the implicit commit.

Although the work process does not have to wait for the response, the user does have to wait. The RFC client application stops until the response is provided by the server and the result is transferred to the user via the user interface. This RFC technology is therefore called *synchronous RFC (sRFC)*. Synchronous means that the client application waits for the response and only continues once the response has been received. Asynchronous techniques have the advantage that the client application can continue even if the RFC is not finished yet. We call this advantage of asynchronous techniques *decoupling* because the client can continue independently of the immediate result from the target server.

Moreover, you will have noticed that up to this point, we have used RFM only for reading data from the RFC server, and not for writing to it. For database **changes**, it is important to ensure that execution happens only once, even in the case of errors. Asynchronous processing can ensure this and we describe this as the quality *exactly once*. We will now discuss the asynchronous part of the RFC story.

1.13   Introducing asynchronous techniques

What we have discussed so far is the synchronous RFC (sRFC); however, there are additional flavors of the RFC statement which are part of *asynchronous processing*.

Interaction pattern

 We refer to synchronous and asynchronous processing as two different *interaction patterns*. Synchronous means that the sender will receive a response to the request but is blocked until then. Asynchronous means that the sender does not wait for an answer from the target and the execution of the application continues.

The aspects of asynchronous processing are as follows:

▶ *No direct response*: the client application sends a request but does not get a direct (business) response—therefore, asynchronous processing is not typically used for reading data from the server

▶ *Decoupling*: the client processing can continue after the RFC statement regardless of whether the server has finished the execution—even regardless of whether the server was reached at all

▶ *Guaranteed delivery*: the delivery of the request data is ensured even if the target system is temporarily not available or if the connection breaks

▶ Exactly once (EO): the database changes in the target system are executed only once, even if identical data is received twice due to an intermediate broken connection

▶ *Exactly once in order (EOIO)*: if required, the sender can put several data packages into a queue and the receiver will follow that defined order while processing the data

These characteristics make asynchronous processing the technique of choice for database changes—that is, for the execution of any RFM that will write to the database.

The advantage is that the ABAP runtime provides the characteristics listed above, so you do not have to do anything here. For example, your coding does not have to use a separate call to check whether the server has successfully processed the data.

Quality of Service (QoS)

 The message processing of *SAP Process Integration* (PI) and *Process Orchestration* is categorized by an attribute called *Quality of Service (QoS)*. For asynchronous processing, the QoS can be exactly-once and exactly-once-in-order. These terms apply for RFC processing as well. The synchronous RFC is adequate to QoS *best-effort*.

For requesting data from the target system, the synchronous RFC is sufficient, as the number of times (i.e., once only or several times) the call is executed is irrelevant. An sRFC offers no specific error handling in the case of a loss of connection—your application will simply have to repeat the call. Because the call does not change anything in the target system, it does not matter whether you execute the call once or several times. The only impact is on the user, who may have to wait a bit longer before getting the result.

Note that the general term asynchronous processing (with RFC) does not mean *asynchronous RFC (aRFC)*—there is a semantic obstacle here!

Semantic trap

 The characteristics of asynchronous processing listed above do **not** apply to a specific member of the RFC family that unfortunately carries the name asynchronous RFC (aRFC). This was introduced long ago and does not relate to the characteristics of asynchronous processing. The aRFC only decouples the request from the response to avoid waiting for the answer. It does **not**, however, ensure guaranteed delivery.

As the aRFC is rarely used—and SAP does not recommend using it—we will look at the syntax only briefly.

1. You send the RFC request by extending the RFC statement with STARTING NEW TASK '<taskname>'. As only data is sent at this point, you can only use EXPORTING and TABLES parameters and should handle the RFC exceptions SYSTEM_FAILURE and COMMUNICATION_FAILURE.

2. You need a form routine in your application (as a callback routine) to receive the results of the RFM (or to handle RFC exceptions). The routine is defined as FORM <formname> using T. To process the response from the RFM, the ABAP runtime will start the form (passing the task name to the parameter T). Inside the form, you handle the response part of the RFC using the statement RECEIVE RESULTS FROM FUNCTION '<name_of_RFM>' and handle the blocks IMPORTING, TABLES, EXCEPTIONS.

3. Finally, you have to include the statement WAIT UNTIL <logexp> in your application. This will put your application in a waiting state so that it can receive the RFC response and execute the form. In the form, you have to set the logical expression <logexp> to true.

Let us reiterate why the characteristics of asynchronous processing are so important for database changes. If you intend to execute an RFM that will execute database changes and the connection breaks during the (synchronous) RFC, you do not know whether the target system has already submitted the changes or not. With asynchronous processing, the ABAP runtime will do the job for you: it will repeat the call and will (in conjunction with the target system) ensure that the data is stored only once (exactly once). It does this even if the data from the first call was already stored in the database before the connection broke.

RFM attributes (continued)

 Note that you will not find an attribute in the Function Builder for an RFM stating whether it can be called synchronously or asynchronously—technically, both are possible. The client application determines whether a call is executed synchronously or asynchronously. It is useless to send an asynchronous call to an RFM that only returns data but does not change the database.

65

Now it is time to implement the asynchronous RFC technique.

1.14 Using background RFC (bgRFC)

The *background RFC (bgRFC)* is the preferred and recommended choice for asynchronous processing with RFC.

---

bgRFC versus tRFC and qRFC

 Two other members of the RFC family allow asynchronous processing as well: *transactional RFC (tRFC)* and *queued RFC (qRFC)*. However, bgRFC is the successor to tRFC and qRFC, offering both exactly-once and exactly-once-in-order processing. Compared to the tRFC and qRFC, the bgRFC shows better performance and offers a common object-oriented approach. Knowledge about the tRFC and qRFC (discussed in Section 1.24) is therefore relevant only for analyzing and understanding existing applications.

Unlike the other RFC statements, the bgRFC implementation includes object-oriented statements. Nevertheless, the call itself is simply the extension of the CALL FUNCTION statement with IN BACKGROUND UNIT but omitting the addition DESTINATION.

The central object for the bgRFC implementation is the *destination* object—it is not an RFC destination, but is bound to an RFC destination. All RFC calls related to this destination object are thus bound to the respective target system. The destination object offers a method for creating a *unit* object, which you use in turn to collect RFC calls for the target system.

The sequence is as follows:

- ▶ Create a destination object, referencing an RFC destination
- ▶ Create a unit object from the destination object
- ▶ Add the unit object to the CALL FUNCTION statement by appending it with IN BACKGROUND UNIT

▶ Optional: do further bgRFC calls

▶ Close the unit with an explicit `COMMIT WORK` statement

The definition of the unit object decides whether the calls are handled exactly-once, or as a sequence exactly-once-in-order. We will start with a section on exactly-once, and will extend this to an example on exactly-once-in-order later.

COMMIT WORK bundles calls

 The `COMMIT WORK` statement is required to ensure that the ABAP runtime puts the calls to the outbound queue for processing. For the bgRFC in particular, this means that the `CALL FUNCTION` statement (with the addition `IN BACKGROUND UNIT`) does not open a remote connection. The source system handles the call and stores the data.

To familiarize ourselves with the bgRFC, we will start with the rather technical RFM STFC_RETURN_DATA. It fills a field of table TCPIC with arbitrary text, as you can verify with a local test in the target system. This approach allows us to focus on the bgRFC steps first. Later, we will create our own RFM that creates data for a new athlete and we will use a bgRFC to execute it remotely.

Use transaction SM59 to set up the existing RFC destination FIRSTDEST for using bgRFC. On the SPECIAL OPTIONS tab, set the option TRANSFER PROTOCOL to *Classic with bgRFC*, as shown in Figure 1.35. Note that the RFC destination can still be used for sRFC without limitations.

The bgRFC also requires some configuration in the system. The following section briefly describes the steps required if the configuration is missing in your system.

Now create a client application to call RFM STFC_RETURN_DATA via bgRFC. Keep in mind that due to the object-oriented approach, we need a `TRY/CATCH` block.

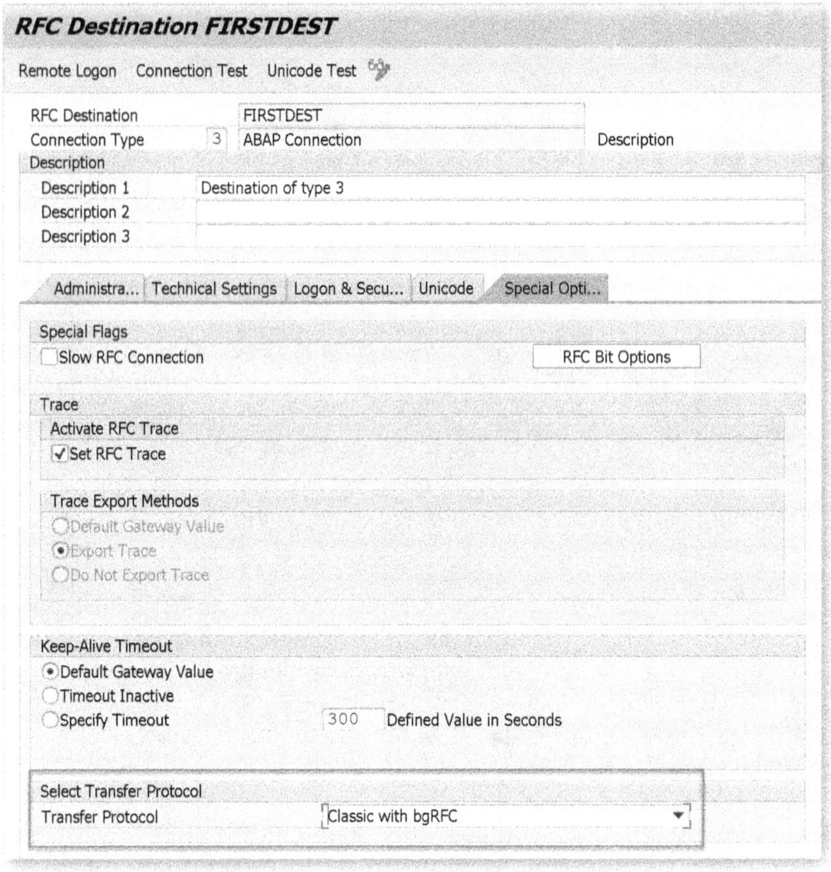

Figure 1.35: Special option "with bgRFC" for RFC destination

Listing 1.9 shows the sequence as well as the interfaces and types used.

```
REPORT z_bgrfc_intro.

PARAMETERS:
pa_dest TYPE bgrfc_dest_name_outbound DEFAULT 'FIRSTDEST',
pa_dat(72) DEFAULT 'No comment' LOWER CASE.

DATA:
gv_action   LIKE sy-input VALUE 'F',
gv_err_fnum LIKE arfcrstate-arfcluwcnt VALUE space,
gs_tcpicdat TYPE abaptext,
```

```
gt_tcpicdat TYPE TABLE OF abaptext.

DATA:
gv_dest TYPE REF TO if_bgrfc_destination_outbound,
go_unit TYPE REF TO if_trfc_unit_outbound,
ge_invalid_dest TYPE REF TO cx_bgrfc_invalid_destination.

CONCATENATE
pa_dat '(created:' sy-uzeit ')'
into gs_tcpicdat SEPARATED BY SPACE.
APPEND gs_tcpicdat TO gt_tcpicdat.

TRY.

gv_dest =
cl_bgrfc_destination_outbound=>create( pa_dest ).
go_unit = gv_dest->create_trfc_unit( ).

  CALL FUNCTION 'STFC_RETURN_DATA'
    IN BACKGROUND UNIT go_unit
        EXPORTING
            action  = gv_action
            err_fnum = gv_err_fnum
        TABLES
            tcpicdat = gt_tcpicdat.
  IF sy-subrc NE 0.
    WRITE: 'UNEXPECTED ERROR'.
    STOP.
  ENDIF.
CATCH cx_bgrfc_invalid_destination INTO ge_invalid_dest.
  WRITE ge_invalid_dest->get_text( ).
  EXIT.
ENDTRY.

COMMIT WORK.
WRITE 'COMMIT WORK done'.
```

Listing 1.9 Report Z_BGRFC_INTRO with tRFC unit

Execute the client report and use the Data Browser (transaction SE16) in the target system to check whether the data was stored in table TCPIC.

The benefit of this simple example is that the table entries include time stamps: the client's data creation time (part of our data, column BUFF-ER) and the server storing time (column UZEIT)—see Figure 1.36. Note that the text is not displayed immediately, as the transmission is decoupled from the CALL FUNCTION statement.

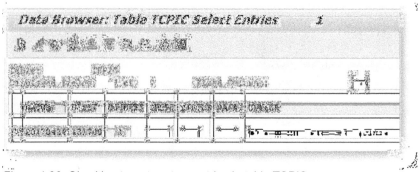

Figure 1.36: Checking target system entries in table TCPIC

If the table entry does not appear even after a while (depending on the parameter WAIT PER UNIT (S) shown later in Figure 1.38), the scheduler configuration for sending the unit is missing.

bgRFC processing sequence

 With the bgRFC call and the COMMIT WORK statement, the data is ready to be processed. The client application then continues to work, independently of the data delivery, as bgRFC is an asynchronous technique. The scheduler in the client system (configuration is covered in the next section) passes the data to the target system which then processes the data and returns the processing status to the client system. If the target system is not accessible, the delivery is rescheduled.

The following sections explain how to create a scheduler configuration for the bgRFC and how to monitor the bgRFC execution.

1.15 Configuring the system for bgRFC

Use transaction SBGRFCCONF to configure the supervisor destination and an outbound scheduler for calls using your RFC destination.

Supervisor destination

The supervisor destination is responsible for transferring bgRFC configuration across the application server (instances) of the local system.

Switch to the last tab DEFINE SUPERVISOR DEST. and use the icon (outlined) to create a new RFC destination (see Figure 1.37).

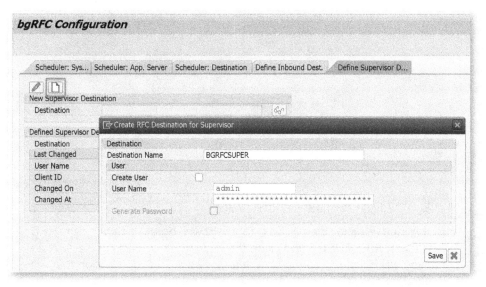

Figure 1.37: Creating the supervisor destination in transaction SBGRFCCONF

In the dialog box, reference an existing user from your local system with its password or use the checkbox CREATE USER to create a new user. Click SAVE in the dialog box and save again by clicking SAVE in the navigation area.

Instead of creating a new supervisor destination, you can reference an existing RFC destination. However, supervisor destinations must not have entries for an application server or instance number.

Outbound scheduler

Now choose the SCHEDULER: DESTINATION tab, choose the icon to create a new destination, and click OUTBOUND to create a configuration entry for an RFC destination, as depicted in Figure 1.38.

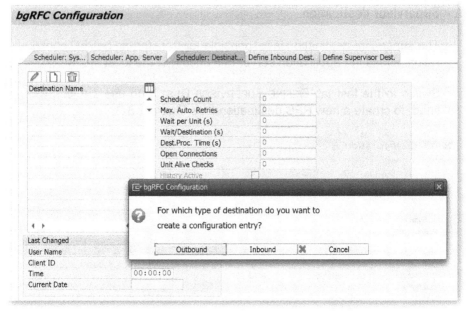

Figure 1.38: Creating a bgRFC scheduler for an RFC destination

In the subsequent dialog box (not shown here), select your RFC destination *FIRSTDEST* and close the dialog box by clicking SAVE. Note that you will have to create a scheduler for each RFC destination that will be used for a bgRFC.

After saving the scheduler configuration, it may take a while before any unit that was created is sent, depending on the value for the parameter WAIT PER UNIT (S) (visible in Figure 1.38 but without a value).

For the target system, no bgRFC-specific configuration is required for the standard case.

1.16 Monitoring bgRFC processing

You monitor the bgRFC units with transaction SBGRFCMON in the source system. The units are listed by the RFC destination to which they were assigned. The selection screen offers several filters, such as inbound or outbound units, RFC destination, and many more (not shown here). Execute the monitor to find your unit listed under the RFC destination *FIRSTDEST*. You can select your unit and use the magnifier icon to see details of the unit, such as the NAME of FIRST FUNCTION MODULE, client program name (TCODE/PROGRAM), etc., as shown in Figure 1.39.

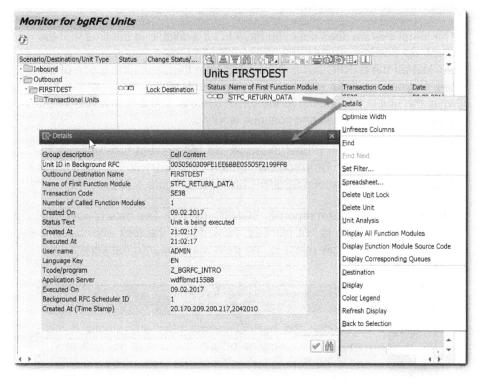

Figure 1.39: bgRFC monitoring in transaction SBGRFCMON with unit details

Why "first function module"? This is because you can bundle several calls into one LUW, even for different RFMs.

1.17 Checking bgRFC guaranteed delivery

Does the overhead for the bgRFC implementation pay off? Yes, because it assures guaranteed delivery of data. If the connection to the target system breaks, you do not have to check whether the data was stored in the target system because this is all handled by the ABAP runtime. The client system repeats the call until it receives confirmation from the target system. On the other hand, the target system ensures that the data is stored only once, even if it receives the same data again. This is quality of service exactly once, and it is ensured by a unique number for each data unit, the *unit ID*, shown in Figure 1.39.

The target system does not even have to be available at the time that the client application creates the data unit. The client application is not blocked as the bgRFC call is decoupled from the actual execution of the call. As you may have experienced, your client application is not blocked while the unit is transmitted to the target system. You can exit your client application after the call and continue working.

Let us check this with a brief exercise: we will prevent data delivery by clicking the Lock Destination button for our RFC destination FIRSTDEST in transaction SBGRFCMON (see Figure 1.39).

Now execute your client report Z_BGRFC_INTRO. The data is not delivered but your report is not blocked. Now delete the lock and create a second call. After a few minutes, the data will appear in the server database table TCPIC.

No magic

 Of course, the bgRFC cannot offer any magic: if the target is and remains offline, the unit is not delivered. And if the data is inconsistent and rejected by the RFM, it will not be stored either. We will examine this situation later.

The next aspect to consider is the sequence in which the data is stored. Even if you do not lock the destination and you execute several calls, you will see that the client sequence is not retained in the target system.

You can compare the time stamps for the send and receive operations in table TCPIC.

So, the bgRFC unit delivery is guaranteed but the sequence in which units are processed in the target does not follow the sequence creation in the client. The sequence may not be relevant for most scenarios. Scenarios that require a sequence to be followed can use the bgRFC with a defined sequence (bgRFC of type qRFC unit). A bgRFC of type qRFC unit fulfills the requirements of quality of service exactly-once-in-order.

1.18 Using queues for bgRFC

Using queues for bgRFC allows you to determine the sequence in which the data units are sent to the target system. For our example report used above, this is not necessary. However, you can imagine cases in which some data has to be created in the target system as a prerequisite for further data that depends on it.

Units are assigned to processing queues in which the sequence is FIFO—first in, first out.

Another important aspect to consider is performance: a sequence will create less load on the target system than several calls in parallel. The bgRFC even allows you to define an inbound queue in the target system for sequential processing from several client systems (not shown here).

You define the queue for the units in the client system and the bgRFC unit references type if_qrfc_unit_outbound. In addition, you have to consider a queue definition and add the queue name of this definition to the unit. Two additional exceptions concerning duplicate queue names and invalid queue names must also be captured.

Listing 1.10 implements the bgRFC with qRFC units.

```
REPORT z_bgrfc_qrfc_unit.

PARAMETERS:
pa_dest TYPE bgrfc_dest_name_outbound DEFAULT 'FIRSTDEST',
pa_dat(72) DEFAULT 'No comment' LOWER CASE,
pa_qn(10) DEFAULT 'QNAME' LOWER CASE.
```

```
DATA:
gv_action   LIKE sy-input VALUE 'F',
gv_err_fnum LIKE arfcrstate-arfcluwcnt VALUE space,
gs_tcpicdat TYPE abaptext,
gt_tcpicdat TYPE TABLE OF abaptext.

DATA:
gv_dest TYPE REF TO if_bgrfc_destination_outbound,
go_unit TYPE REF TO if_qrfc_unit_outbound,  " qRFC unit
gv_qn TYPE qrfc_queue_name,
ge_invalid_dest TYPE REF TO cx_bgrfc_invalid_destination,
ge_invalid_qname TYPE REF TO cx_qrfc_invalid_queue_name,
ge_dupl_qname TYPE REF TO CX_QRFC_DUPLICATE_QUEUE_NAME,
lock_id        TYPE bgrfc_lock_id.

CONCATENATE pa_dat '(created:' sy-uzeit ')'
into gs_tcpicdat SEPARATED BY SPACE.
APPEND gs_tcpicdat TO gt_tcpicdat.

TRANSLATE pa_qn TO UPPER CASE.
gv_qn = pa_qn.

TRY.

gv_dest =
cl_bgrfc_destination_outbound=>create( pa_dest ).
go_unit = gv_dest->create_qrfc_unit( ).  "create qRFC unit

   CALL FUNCTION 'STFC_RETURN_DATA'
    IN BACKGROUND UNIT go_unit
       EXPORTING
            action  = gv_action
            err_fnum = gv_err_fnum
        TABLES
            tcpicdat = gt_tcpicdat.
   IF sy-subrc NE 0.
     WRITE: 'UNEXPECTED ERROR'.
     STOP.
   ENDIF.
   go_unit->add_queue_name_outbound( gv_qn ).
```

```
CATCH cx_bgrfc_invalid_destination INTO ge_invalid_dest.
  WRITE ge_invalid_dest->get_text( ).
  EXIT.
CATCH cx_qrfc_invalid_queue_name INTO ge_invalid_qname.
  WRITE ge_invalid_qname->get_text( ).
  EXIT.
CATCH cx_qrfc_duplicate_queue_name INTO ge_dupl_qname.
  WRITE ge_dupl_qname->get_text( ).
  EXIT.
ENDTRY.

COMMIT WORK.
WRITE 'Commit work done'.
```

Listing 1.10: bgRFC with qRFC unit using queues

1.19 Creating RFMs to change data

Returning to our custom development, let us now create our next customer-specific RFM. This RFM will create data for a new athlete, so it will change data on the target database. For this purpose, we have to think about the *ABAP update technique*.

ABAP update technique

 Firstly, the general concept of the *ABAP update technique* means that the OpenSQL statements (to change the database) are not executed directly. Instead, the concept comprises a local call to an *update function module* with the addition IN UPDATE TASK, followed later by a COMMIT WORK statement. The update function module includes the OpenSQL statement. The call to the update function module does not lead to immediate execution of the module. Instead, the data of the call is stored in internal tables (special section of the database called VBLOG). The transfer to the database only takes place once the COMMIT WORK statement has been triggered. Pending update requests can be monitored in transaction SM13.

To optimize performance, the OpenSQL statement inside the update function module can be encapsulated in a form routine. The form routine is called with the addition `ON COMMIT`, and thereby, datasets are first passed to an internal buffer table. The form is then executed only once, when the `COMMIT WORK` statement is triggered, and it stores all datasets from the buffer table.

Thinking about the update technique in ABAP, we will create an RFM and an update function module. The sequence is depicted in Figure 1.40. The data to be written to the database is stored intermediately in a specific section of the database called VBLOG.

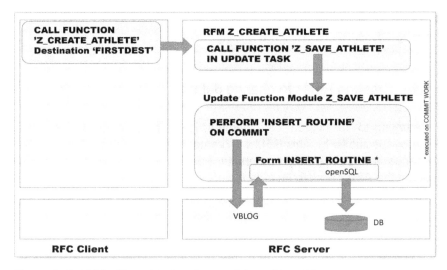

Figure 1.40: RFM with update function module and insert form

Our object creation sequence follows the sequence of calls in Figure 1.40 above: we start by creating the RFM, then we create the update function module, from which we create the form routine.

RFM attributes (continued)

Note that you will not find a dedicated attribute in the Function Builder for an RFM stating whether the module uses an update technique.

78

1. Create the RFM

Let's go: create a new function module Z_CREATE_ATHLETE as part of the existing function group ZSPORTS with the attribute REMOTE-ENABLED. For the short text, use the prefix RFM as before. Maintain the parameters shown in Listing 1.11 for the interface section.

```
FUNCTION Z_CREATE_ATHLETE.
*"----------------------------------------------------------
*"*"Local Interface:
*"  IMPORTING
*"     VALUE(I_ATHLETE_NAME) TYPE  ZNAME
*"     VALUE(I_DATE_OF_BIRTH) TYPE  ZBIRTHDATE
*"     VALUE(I_COUNTRY) TYPE  LAND1
*"     VALUE(I_DO_COMMIT) TYPE  CHAR01
*"  EXPORTING
*"     VALUE(E_ATHLETE_ID) TYPE  ZATHLETE-ATHLETE_ID
*"  EXCEPTIONS
*"      MISSING_AUTHORIZATION
*"      INVALID_DATA
*"      OBJECT_LOCKED
*"----------------------------------------------------------
```

Listing 1.11: Interface section of RFM Z_CREATE_ATHLETE

We provide the name, the date of birth, and the country of the athlete—the athlete ID will be provided internally, using the internal number range. In addition, we introduce an interface parameter to decide whether the COMMIT WORK statement will be executed by the RFM. The statement is required to write the data to the database; however, a test call without execution of a COMMIT WORK statement will allow us to test only the input values without writing to the database. This approach also allows us to bundle several calls and to only provide the COMMIT WORK statement in the last RFC. This approach allows a performant processing of mass data.

The sequence of steps inside the RFM is as follows:

1. Authorization check

2. Consistency check for import parameters

3. Pass import parametes to internal variables

4. Create database lock

5. Get next athlete number

6. Call update function module, provide parameters

7. Commit work

Listing 1.12 shows the respective coding proposal.

```
DATA: lv_athlete_id TYPE zathlete-athlete_id,
      lv_land TYPE land1.

* Authorization check
  AUTHORITY-CHECK OBJECT 'ZATHLETE'
           ID 'ACTVT' FIELD '01'.
  IF sy-subrc NE 0.
    MESSAGE e002(zsports) RAISING missing_authorization.
  ENDIF.

*Consistency checks
  IF i_athlete_name IS INITIAL OR
     i_date_of_birth IS INITIAL OR
     i_country       IS INITIAL .
    MESSAGE e001(zsports) RAISING invalid_data.
  ENDIF.

  CALL FUNCTION 'DATE_CHECK_PLAUSIBILITY'
    EXPORTING
      date                    = i_date_of_birth
    EXCEPTIONS
      plausibility_check_failed = 1
      OTHERS                  = 2.
  IF sy-subrc NE 0.
    MESSAGE e003(zsports) WITH 'Date format wrong'
      RAISING invalid_data.
  ENDIF.

  SELECT SINGLE land1 FROM t005 INTO lv_land
                 WHERE land1 = i_country.
```

```
    IF sy-subrc NE 0.
      MESSAGE e003(zsports) WITH 'country not found'
      RAISING invalid_data.
    ENDIF.

*   Next steps only if commit is wanted
    IF i_do_commit = 'X'.

*  Create database lock
      CALL FUNCTION 'ENQUEUE_EZATHLETE'
        EXPORTING
*         MODE_ZATHLETE   = 'E'
          mandt           = sy-mandt
        EXCEPTIONS
          foreign_lock    = 1
          system_failure  = 2
          OTHERS          = 3.
      IF sy-subrc <> 0.
        MESSAGE e005(zsports) RAISING object_locked.
      ENDIF.

      CALL FUNCTION 'NUMBER_GET_NEXT'
        EXPORTING
          nr_range_nr            = '1'
          object                 = 'ZATHLETE'
        IMPORTING
          number                 = lv_athlete_id
        EXCEPTIONS
          interval_not_found     = 1
          number_range_not_intern = 2
          object_not_found       = 3
          quantity_is_0          = 4
          quantity_is_not_1      = 5
          interval_overflow      = 6
          buffer_overflow        = 7
          OTHERS                 = 8.
      IF sy-subrc <> 0.
        MESSAGE e001(zsports) WITH sy-subrc.
      ENDIF.
```

```
* Call update function module, provide parameters
    CALL FUNCTION 'Z_SAVE_ATHLETE'
      IN UPDATE TASK
      EXPORTING
        i_athlete_name  = i_athlete_name
        i_date_of_birth = i_date_of_birth
        i_country       = i_country
        i_athlete_id    = lv_athlete_id.

    e_athlete_id = lv_athlete_id.
    COMMIT WORK.
  ENDIF.


ENDFUNCTION.
```

Listing 1.12: Implementation of RFM Z_CREATE_ATHLETE

2. Create update function module

You can create the update function module by double-clicking the respective `CALL FUNCTION` statement and using the forward navigation. You can follow this approach later as well, when creating the form routine from inside the update function module.

On the ATTRIBUTES tab, under PROCESSING TYPE, select UPDATE MODULE, as shown in Figure 1.41, and use a prefix *UPD* for the short text.

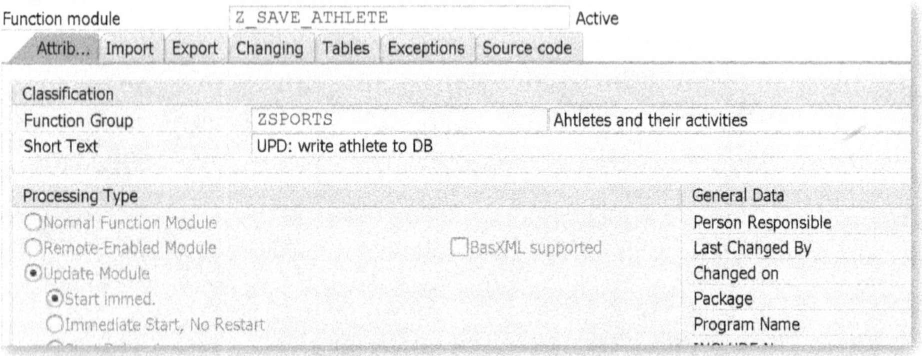

Figure 1.41: Attributes of update function module Z_SAVE_ATHLETE

In the update function module, we use a local call to the module NUM-BER_GET_NEXT to obtain the next athlete ID. Then, instead of writing the data to the database, we fill a buffer table with the data for the new athlete. Finally, the form routine is called with the addition ON COMMIT. This determines that the routine is called only once, after the closing COMMIT WORK statement. It then writes the data from the buffer table (each line is one new athlete) to the database, which makes the overall process very performant. See Listing 1.13 for the coding proposal for the update function module.

```
FUNCTION z_save_athlete.
*"----------------------------------------------------------
*"*"Update Function Module:
*"
*"*"Local Interface:
*"  IMPORTING
*"     VALUE(I_ATHLETE_NAME) TYPE   ZNAME
*"     VALUE(I_DATE_OF_BIRTH) TYPE   ZBIRTHDATE
*"     VALUE(I_COUNTRY) TYPE   LAND1
*"     VALUE(I_ATHLETE_ID) TYPE   ZATHLETE-ATHLETE_ID
*"----------------------------------------------------------

  gs_athlete-date_of_birth = i_date_of_birth.
  gs_athlete-name          = i_athlete_name.
  gs_athlete-country       = i_country.
  gs_athlete-athlete_id    = i_athlete_id.

* Append new athlete to buffer table
  APPEND gs_athlete TO gt_athlete_buffer.

  PERFORM insert_athlete ON COMMIT.

ENDFUNCTION.
```

Listing 1.13: Implementation of update function module Z_SAVE_ATHLETE

We use the TOP include to define the table buffer and the structure, as shown in Listing 1.14.

```
FUNCTION-POOL ZSPORTS.          "MESSAGE-ID ..
Data: gs_athlete type zathlete,
gt_athlete_buffer type table of zathlete.
* INCLUDE LZSPORTSD...           " Local class definition
```

Listing 1.14: Declaration of global variables in TOP include

The form is put into the include LZSPORTSF01, as shown in Listing
1.15.

```
*--------------------------------------------------------*
***INCLUDE LZSPORTSF01 .
*--------------------------------------------------------*
*&-------------------------------------------------------*
*&      Form  INSERT_ACTIVITY
*&-------------------------------------------------------
FORM insert_athlete.
insert zathlete from table gt_athlete_buffer.
  IF sy-subrc NE 0.
    MESSAGE e001(zsports) WITH 'db insert error: athlete'.
  ENDIF.
ENDFORM.                          " INSERT_ATHLETE
```

Listing 1.15: Include LZSPORTSF01

At this point, you may wonder whether a naming convention might be
useful, to distinguish local modules from RFMs. In our example, we use
only the short text to do this. The indication can be put into the name as
well, for example, Z_RFM_CREATE_ATHLETE—but this would extend
the name. Therefore, we use a prefix for the short text. The short texts
are visible in the object list of the function group, see Figure 1.42.

ZSPORTS	Modules for athletes
Function Modules	
· Z_ATHLETES_LIST	RFM: list all athletes
· Z_ATHLETE_READ_DETAILS	RFM: read details on athlete
· Z_CREATE_ATHLETE	RFM: create new athlete
· Z_SAVE_ATHLETE	UPD: save athlete data
Subroutines	
· INSERT_ATHLETE	
Includes	
· LZSPORTSF01	Include LZSPORTSF01
· LZSPORTSTOP	
· LZSPORTSUXX	LZSPORTSUXX

Figure 1.42: Object list of function group ZSPORTS

COMMIT WORK in RFM

 How about using an existing RFM to update the database: does it contain the COMMIT WORK statement or not? Not all such RFMs have such an obvious parameter named I_DO_COMMIT. And there is no such attribute for a function module that explains whether the module requires an external COMMIT WORK statement.

You can check the documentation (if there is any) or read the code—which can be a complex task. However, the best practice is to perform a test in the Function Builder, as described in the following section.

1.20 Testing RFMs with database changes

Imagine that you want to use an existing RFM that changes the database. How do you know whether it requires an external COMMIT WORK statement because it uses the update technique but does not execute the COMMIT WORK statement as part of the module source code? You can get a good indication by testing the RFM in the Function Builder.

If you execute the RFM in the Function Builder and it finishes without an error message, you can check whether the changes were written to the database. If the result was not written to the database, this is an indication that the COMMIT WORK statement is not part of the RFM and is therefore missing.

You can reproduce this with a test of your brand new RFM Z_CREATE_ ATHLETE by keeping the default value SPACE for the parameter I_DO_COMMIT.

OK—that part was the negative confirmation. But how about vice versa: you want to test such an RFM (which requires an external COMMIT WORK statement) and want to see that your data is successfully stored at database level. The problem is that the test in the Function Builder does not allow you to submit a concluding COMMIT WORK statement.

There are two ways to achieve our goal: either we use the *Extended Computer Aided Test Tool (eCATT)*—we will look at this in the next section—or we use a *test sequence* in the Function Builder which allows us to couple two module calls in a sequence. The first call is for the RFM and the second is for a module executing the COMMIT WORK statement.

To create a test sequence, start from the display of the RFM and choose FUNCTION MODULE • EXECUTE • TEST SEQUENCES. A dialog box appears allowing you to enter the names of the modules to be executed in a sequence, see Figure 1.43.

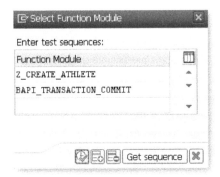

Figure 1.43: Test sequence for RFM with database changes

The first module is our RFM but what about the second one: BA-PI_TRANSACTION_COMMIT? It is a module that contains no more than the COMMIT WORK statement. (We will come back to this topic later in the chapter on *BAPIs*.)

Click ⏪ to proceed and you will experience two function module tests in a sequence. Make sure you keep the parameter I_DO_COMMIT set to the default value (SPACE) for the first test. The second module does not require any input; simply execute the test and return to the RFM. Now check the database table ZATHLETE: the data was stored, which means that both modules were executed as one LUW. This is the proof that an external COMMIT WORK statement is required for the RFM.

Note that we have done this exercise for our custom RFM for which we already know that the requirement applies but the procedure applies to any RFM that you do not know by heart.

1.21 Testing an RFM with eCATT

Before we turn to the client system to create the bgRFC client application that targets our new RFM, let us extend our knowledge on testing RFMs.

You can skip this section now and study it later if you like. But remember that testing with eCATT allows remote testing of a custom RFM from the client. This is not possible with the test environment of the Function Builder.

The Function Builder test environment does allow a remote connection. The prerequisite for this, however, is that the RFM interface exists locally in the client as well to allow a remote execution. However, custom-built RFMs typically exist only in the target system, not in each client system.

1.21.1 Introduction to eCATT

eCATT is the abbreviation for Extended Computer Aided Test Tool. It offers a variety of use cases; we will focus only on interface testing for RFMs. The main element of such a test is the *test script*; it contains ABAP statements written in a specific syntax called *Inline ABAP*.

The sequence of test preparation for a given RFM is as follows:

1) Create a system data container

2) Create a test script

3) Add a command to the test script

4) Add COMMIT WORK statement (optional)

The *system data container* decouples the test script **coding** from the connectivity **configuration**. This is like the approach for RFC technology: an RFC client application is implemented and transported as an ABAP object but the connectivity configuration is kept separately in an RFC destination.

No target repository access for eCATT

 The eCATT environment cannot read the target interface remotely from the client. There is no global repository for RFMs and our RFM interface exists only in the target.

So how can we test a custom RFM from a client system where the interface does not exist? The approach is to first create the test script locally in the target system which contains the RFM and then transport the test script to the client system. As the test script contains the RFM interface information, the test script can then be executed successfully in the client system.

Therefore, we start in the target system in which the system data container references the local system. Later, after we have transported the test script to the client system, we will execute the same test script using a new, local system data container that points to the target system.

1.21.2 eCATT in the target system

In the target system, use transaction SECATT to start eCATT. In the object section on the left-hand side of the entry screen, you can view existing objects as well as create new objects, see Figure 1.44.

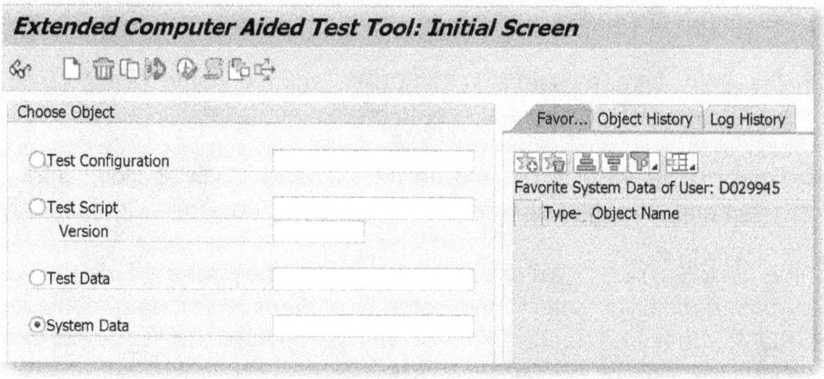

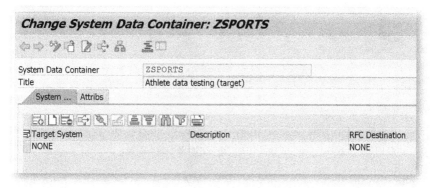

Figure 1.44: eCATT initial screen

1) Create a system data container

On the entry screen, select SYSTEM DATA, enter a name (*ZSPORTS*), and press F5 to open the system data maintenance screen.

On the ATTRIBUTES tab, enter a title such as *Athlete data testing* and switch to the SYSTEM DATA tab. There is already one entry, *NONE*, referencing the predefined RFC destination with the same name (see Figure 1.45). This allows a local test.

Figure 1.45: eCATT system data container ZSPORTS in the target system

Now save the system data container, provide a package, and return to the eCATT entry screen. The system data container will be referenced in the script definition and used for the test script execution later.

2) Create a test script

On the entry screen, select TEST SCRIPT, enter a name (*ZAHTLETE_ CREATE_SCRIPT*), and press [F5] to create the script.

We start on the ATTRIBUTES tab. In the GENERAL DATA section, enter a short text and an application component (e.g., *BC* for Basis Component).

In the MAINTENANCE SYSTEM area, use the input help for the SYSTEMDATA CONTAINER field to select and reference the system data container *ZSPORTS* that we created in the previous step. Use the [F4] input help to choose *NONE* for the TARGET SYSTEM field, as shown in Figure 1.46.

Change Test Script: ZATHLETE_CREATE_SCRIPT (1)

Pattern	Pretty Printer	

Test Script	ZATHLETE_CREATE_SCRIPT	Version	1
Title	Test to create athlete data locally via RFM		

E... Attribu...

General ... Versioning Data Extras Restrictions

Header Data

Title	Test to create athlete data locally via RFM	
Package	$TMP	
Person Responsible	ADMIN	ADMIN
Application Component	BC	Basis Components

Maintenance System

SystemData Container	ZSPORTS	
Target System	NONE	

Figure 1.46: eCATT test script attributes

The first tab, EDITOR, will contain the ABAP inline code but we will work on that later. Save your script and provide a package.

Although our script does not contain any code yet, we execute it for a first test. You can start the test from the detailed view of the test script. Press [F8] to see the START OPTIONS and then press [F8] again. The log display should then show a green line indicating success. If an error appears (such as an authorization issue, see below), fix it before proceeding. Then return to your test script.

---

eCATT restrictions in the client

 The settings for an ABAP client can restrict the execution of test scripts. Check the client settings in transaction SCC4 for the option CATT AND ECATT RESTRICTIONS. (Note that *CATT* is the predecessor of eCATT.) If the execution is not allowed, the test of the empty test script will fail.

3) Add a command to the test script

Now we will add the call of our RFM to the test script. You can edit the test script directly, but it is helpful to use the *pattern* function that provides a list of possible statements. In your test script ZATHLETE _CREATE_SCRIPT, on the first tab, EDITOR, choose PATTERN. This opens a dialog box which lists all possible ABAP inline commands. In the GROUP field, select *ALL COMMANDS* and in the COMMAND field, select *FUN* (see Figure 1.47).

🗗 Insert statement		☒
Group	ALL COMMANDS	▼
Command	FUN	▼
Function Module	Z_CREATE_ATHLETE	
Interface	Z_CREATE_ATHLETE_1	
Target System	NONE	▼
	✓ ☒ ⓘ	

Figure 1.47: eCATT pattern insertion for a function module call

Note that we are working in the target system, so the RFM interface does exist. This means that you can use the input help or manually enter the name of your function module *Z_CREATE_ATHLETE*. The test script assigns an internal *interface* name for the function module. Press ⌨Enter to fill the INTERFACE field with a generated string *Z_CREATE _ATHLETE_1*. The TARGET SYSTEM field already contains a value. Now proceed by pressing ⌨Enter again—this closes the dialog box and adds the respective ABAP inline statement listed here to your script (shown in Figure 1.48):

```
FUN ( Z_CREATE_ATHLETE , Z_CREATE_ATHLETE_1 ).
```

Checkbox CREATE PARAMETER

If the CREATE PARAMETER checkbox is offered (this depends on the respective system release), use it to automatically create parameters for the module interface. However, we will also discuss how to create parameters manually.

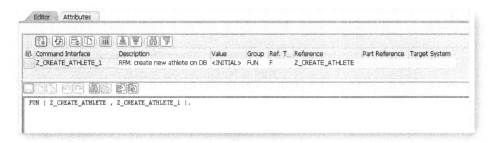

Figure 1.48: eCATT script with ABAP inline statement

Now the script contains a statement, but we cannot provide input values to the function module call yet, as the script as such has no parameters defined. The execution of the test script as it is would fail with the error INVALID_DATA (raised by the function module).

To see the interface, click the COMMAND INTERFACE VALUE icon above the COMMAND INTERFACE row. The interface parameters of our RFM are then listed on the right-hand side, next to the ABAP inline editor (see Figure 1.49).

We have to create script parameters and then assign them to the interface parameters.

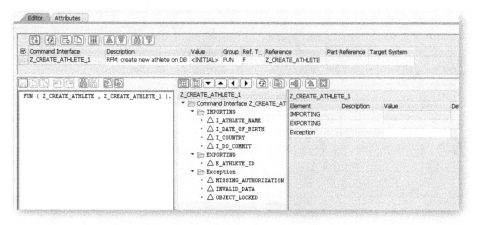

Figure 1.49: eCATT command interface with parameters

To add script parameters, use the ▦ icon to switch from the COMMAND INTERFACE to the PARAMETER display. The third icon ▦ then allows you to add parameters. Create the parameters *ATHLETE_NAME, DATE_OF_BIRTH, COUNTRY* and *DO_COMMIT*. Set their type to *I* for input and set the ABAP TYPE and LENGTH fields accordingly, as shown in Figure 1.50 at ❶. The column PARAMETER REFERENCE allows you to reference parameters but as our ZATHLETE DDIC structure exists only locally in the target system, we omit this step. This way, we can use the script in the RFC client later as well.

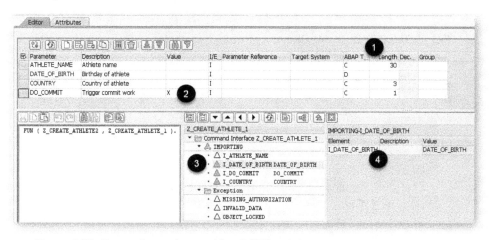

Figure 1.50: Parameter assignment in eCATT script

You can use the VALUE column to set the default values for the test script. As you can see in Figure 1.50 at ❷, the default value was only maintained for the parameter *DO_COMMIT*. We have to maintain the other values when we start the script execution in the START OPTIONS dialog, on the respective PARAMETERS tab.

Before starting the script, we have to connect the script parameters to the input parameters of the RFM. Double-click the interface parameters (❸) and maintain the script parameter in the VALUE field. In Figure 1.50 at ❹, you can see the assignment of the interface parameter (ELEMENT column) *I_DATE_OF_BIRTH* to script parameter (VALUE column) *DATE_OF_BIRTH*. Maintain this connection between script and input parameters for all four parameters. They will then be displayed with a yellow triangle, like *I_ATHLETE_NAME* in Figure 1.50.

Start another test of the script but this time, on the START OPTIONS screen, switch to the second tab PARAMETERS and maintain values for the two parameters *ATHLETE_NAME* and *DATE_OF_BIRTH*. After the execution of the test script, check whether the table ZATHLETE was updated. You can use either transaction SE16 for this check or a local execution of your RFM Z_ATHLETE_READ_DETAILS.

Now execute a sequence of two tests: for the first run, set the parameter *DO_COMMIT* to *SPACE* (as an explicit string). This should determine that the first dataset is not stored on the database. Then, immediately after the first test, execute a second test, this time with parameter *DO_COMMIT* set to *X*. Check the database table afterwards: both datasets are stored! How has that happened?

eCATT and data context

 eCATT tests are executed via RFC—remember the RFC destination NONE, referenced in the system data container. By default, the RFC connection is kept after each call and not closed. Therefore, all calls from the eCATT application are handled in the same context. The first dataset is not lost, even without a `COMMIT_WORK` statement, as the context is still there. Hence, the first dataset is also stored by the `COMMIT_WORK` statement at the end of the second dataset execution.

The START OPTIONS screen offers the checkbox CLOSE RFC CONNEC-TION (in the RFC section) to keep each test execution separate from the others.

You can use the Gateway Monitor (transaction SMGW) to check for the open connection.

To enable the script to be used in the client system, it has to be transported. A shortcut that makes our work easier is to export and import the script instead. Therefore, select TEST SCRIPT • OTHER FEATURES • DOWNLOAD to download the script as a local xml file.

As a side step, let us see how you can provide the COMMIT WORK statement for RFMs that do not trigger this statement internally.

1.21.3 Triggering COMMIT WORK

Some RFMs require an external COMMIT WORK statement and do not offer an input parameter for this. You can extend the script with ABAP coding to trigger such an explicit COMMIT WORK statement. You have to mask the ABAP coding with the tags ABAP and ENDABAP. Listing 1.16 shows the extended script:

```
FUN ( Z_CREATE_ATHLETE , Z_CREATE_ATHLETE_1 ).
ABAP.
COMMIT WORK.
ENDABAP.
```

Listing 1.16: Extended script with COMMIT WORK statement

You can test this by temporarily extending your test script with these statements. Then start the test and overwrite the default value of *DO_COMMIT* with the string *SPACE*. Again, use transaction SE16 (or a local execution of your RFM Z_ATHLETE_READ_DETAILS) to check that the athlete was created. After this test, remove the additional coding from your test script.

95

1.21.4 eCATT in the client system

Now, in the client system, before we import the script from the local file, we will create a system data container. In the client system, use transaction SECATT to start eCATT.

1) Create a system data container

On the entry screen, select SYSTEM DATA, enter a name (*ZSPORTS*), and press ⌐F5⌐ to open the system data maintenance screen.

Naming the system data container

In general, the name of the system data container can be different to the name we have chosen in the target system. After the import of the script, either the system data container has to be adapted in the script, or at least the name of the TARGET SYSTEM in the system data container.

On the ATTRIBUTES tab, maintain a title such as *Athlete data testing (from client to target)* and switch to the SYSTEM DATA tab. You will find the existing entry *NONE*. As the RFM exists only in the target system, it does not make sense to keep this local entry so delete it.

Still on the SYSTEM DATA tab, click 📋 ADD TARGET SYSTEM to add a line to the table. Maintain the name for the entry (*SPORTS*), a short text, and reference the transaction SM59 destination *FIRSTDEST* that points to the target system providing the RFM (see Figure 1.51).

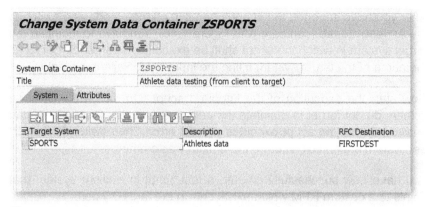

Figure 1.51: eCATT system data container ZSPORTS in the client system

Finally, save the system data container, provide a package, and return to the eCATT entry screen.

2) Import the script

On the eCATT entry screen, choose ECATT OBJECT • OTHER FEATURES • UPLOAD to upload the script from the local xml file. After you have speci-fied the local xml file, a dialog box is shown with details of the script (see Figure 1.52). Confirm it with ⌈Enter⌉.

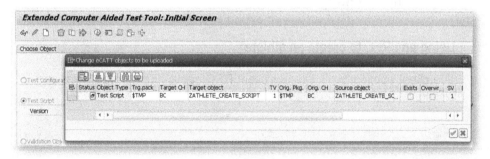

Figure 1.52: Import of eCATT script

After you have imported the script, open it in change mode and switch to the ATTRIBUTES tab (compare with Figure 1.46). You have to maintain the target system in which the script shall be executed, so enter *SPORTS* as the name of the target system using the input help. Save the script.

Now start the execution of the imported script. On the START OPTIONS screen, do not forget to maintain the parameters on the PARAMETERS tab and check that the script executes without error. Then switch to the target system and check whether the athlete was created.

You have now successfully created a test script in a client system that points to a custom RFM which exists only in the target system.

1.22 Comparing synchronous and bgRFC

Now let us create an RFC client application that targets our new function module and creates a new athlete in the target system.

The first step is to discuss and implement the sRFC. We can then implement the bgRFC to ensure exactly-once behavior.

1.22.1 Implementing sRFC

Using an sRFC to create an athlete

The client application is like our client RFC application to read data, see Listing 1.17.

```
REPORT z_create_new_athlete_sync.

PARAMETERS: pa_name(23) LOWER CASE,
pa_bdate TYPE dats DEFAULT sy-datum,
pa_com(1) DEFAULT 'X',
pa_cntry TYPE land1,
pa_dest TYPE rfcdes-rfcdest DEFAULT 'FIRSTDEST'.

DATA: lv_id(12) TYPE n, gv_msg(100).
```

```
*Consistency checks
IF pa_name IS INITIAL OR
  pa_bdate IS INITIAL OR
  pa_cntry IS INITIAL.
  WRITE: 'Missing parameter'.
  EXIT.
ENDIF.

TRY.
  CALL METHOD cl_isu_date_check=>date_check_plausibility
    EXPORTING
      x_date                    = pa_bdate
    EXCEPTIONS
      plausibility_check_failed = 1
      OTHERS                    = 2.
  IF sy-subrc NE 0.
    WRITE: 'Invalid date'.
  ENDIF.
ENDTRY.

CALL FUNCTION 'Z_CREATE_ATHLETE'
  DESTINATION pa_dest
  EXPORTING
    i_athlete_name      = pa_name
    i_date_of_birth     = pa_bdate
    i_country           = pa_cntry
    i_do_commit         = pa_com
  IMPORTING
    e_athlete_id        = lv_id
  EXCEPTIONS
    missing_authorization = 1
    invalid_data          = 2
    object_locked         = 3
    system_failure        = 4  MESSAGE gv_msg
    communication_failure = 5  MESSAGE gv_msg
    OTHERS                = 6.

CASE sy-subrc.
  WHEN 0.
```

```
      WRITE: 'Call done, ', lv_id.
    WHEN 4 OR 5.
      WRITE: 'error:', gv_msg.
    WHEN OTHERS.
      WRITE: 'error: ', sy-subrc.
  ENDCASE.
```

Listing 1.17: sRFC to RFM for an update

It is good practice to include data validation in the client application as this avoids unnecessary calls that will be rejected by the target system.

As a special exercise, let us examine a client application that will send two new athletes to the target system. Let's assume that they belong together, so we want only both or none to be stored. We put these into one LUW by only committing after the second call. Listing 1.18 illustrates the approach.

```
...
CALL FUNCTION 'Z_CREATE_ATHLETE'
DESTINATION pa_dest
  EXPORTING
    i_athlete_name          = 'First Athlete'
    i_date_of_birth         = pa_bdate1
    i_country               = pa_cntry
    i_do_commit             = ''
...
CALL FUNCTION 'Z_CREATE_ATHLETE'
DESTINATION pa_dest
  EXPORTING
    i_athlete_name          = 'Second Athlete'
    i_date_of_birth         = pa_bdate2
    i_country               = pa_cntry
    i_do_commit             = 'X'
...
```

Listing 1.18: Two sRFC calls in one LUW

As the connection is kept for an sRFC, both calls are part of one LUW and stored together. Can we skip the I_DO_COMMIT parameter for the second call as well, and simply execute the COMMIT_WORK statement, just like for bgRFC? Of course not, as this will only be executed locally and not transferred to the target system. For the bgRFC, the required COMMIT_WORK statement is not transferred to the target system either but triggers the execution of the bgRFC units.

Providing an external COMMIT WORK statement for an sRFC

As the last part of our sRFC discussion, let us consider an RFM that requires an external COMMIT WORK statement but does not offer a convenient parameter I_DO_COMMIT. We have to provide the COMMIT WORK statement as a second call via the existing RFC connection. To do this, we would again make use of the RFM which contains the COMMIT WORK statement: BAPI_TRANSACTION_COMMIT (of course, only if the first call is successful). A template for this approach is shown in Listing 1.19.

```
...
CALL FUNCTION 'Z_CREATE_ATHLETE'
DESTINATION pa_dest
  EXPORTING
    i_athlete_name              = 'First Athlete'
    i_date_of_birth             = pa_bdate1
    i_country                   = pa_cntry
    i_do_commit                 = ' '
  ...
CALL FUNCTION 'BAPI_TRANSACTION_COMMIT'
DESTINATION pa_dest
  ...
```

Listing 1.19: Providing a subsequent external COMMIT WORK statement

101

RFC connection allows LUW

Remember that the RFC connection remains open after an sRFC statement as long as the context of the client application exists. This allows us to have two subsequent calls in one LUW.

On the other hand, if we want to separate two RFC statements so that they are not executed via the same connection (and the same LUW), the connection to the remote system must be closed. We can do this by using a local call to function module RFC_CONNECTION_CLOSE after the first call. But keep in mind that this has a negative impact on the performance, as the second call will have to open the connection again.

Now, what happens if the connection breaks for our sRFC client: how do we know if the data has already been processed? There is no easy way to know. Therefore, we will use a bgRFC to ensure exactly-once processing.

1.22.2 Using a bgRFC to create an athlete

No COMMIT WORK statement in an RFM for asynchronous processing

An RFM that is called asynchronously is not allowed to execute a COMMIT WORK statement on its own, as this statement is triggered by the ABAP runtime of the target system automatically. Therefore, we must keep the parameter I_DO_COMMIT initial.

Listing 1.20 shows an example report for the bgRFC call.

```
REPORT z_create_new_athlete_async.

PARAMETERS: pa_name(23) LOWER CASE,
```

102

```abap
pa_bdate TYPE dats DEFAULT sy-datum,
pa_cntry TYPE land1,
pa_dest TYPE rfcdes-rfcdest DEFAULT 'FIRSTDEST'.
data:
gv_dest TYPE ref TO if_bgrfc_destination_outbound,
go_trfc_unit TYPE ref TO if_trfc_unit_outbound,
ge_invalid_dest TYPE ref TO cx_bgrfc_invalid_destination.

DATA: lv_name TYPE c LENGTH 23.

*Consistency checks
  IF pa_name IS INITIAL OR
    pa_bdate IS INITIAL OR
    pa_cntry IS INITIAL.
    WRITE: 'Missing parameter'.
    EXIT.
  ENDIF.

TRY.
CALL METHOD cl_isu_date_check=>date_check_plausibility
  EXPORTING
    x_date                   = pa_bdate
  EXCEPTIONS
    plausibility_check_failed = 1
    others                   = 2.
IF  sy-subrc ne 0.
  WRITE: 'Invalid date'.
  EXIT.
  ENDIF.
ENDTRY.

TRY.
gv_dest =
cl_bgrfc_destination_outbound=>create( pa_dest ).
go_trfc_unit = gv_dest->create_trfc_unit( ).

CALL FUNCTION 'Z_CREATE_ATHLETE'
  IN BACKGROUND UNIT go_trfc_unit
    EXPORTING
    i_athlete_name           = pa_name
    i_date_of_birth          = pa_bdate
```

103

```
     i_country                  = pa_cntry
     i_do_commit                = ''

          .

  IF sy-subrc NE 0.
     WRITE: 'UNEXPECTED ERROR', sy-subrc.
     STOP.
   ENDIF.
       WRITE 'tRFC queue filled'.

CATCH cx_bgrfc_invalid_destination INTO ge_invalid_dest.
  WRITE ge_invalid_dest->get_text( ).
  EXIT.
ENDTRY.

COMMIT WORK.
WRITE 'Commit work done'.
```

Listing 1.20: Asynchronous RFC client application using bgRFC

So, by using a bgRFC, we can be sure that the dataset is created exactly once, even if there are connectivity issues. But what about invalid data that you did not detect in the client? There is no error message for invalid data. To ensure that only valid data is sent, you can potentially combine an sRFC with a subsequent bgRFC. The sRFC first checks whether the data is accepted by the target but does not provide the I_DO_COMMIT. Afterwards, if the call was successful, the bgRFC sends the validated data to be stored in the target. As this is a simple combination of our last two listings, we will only show the principle here (see Listing 1.21). Remember that this combination will not be as performant as only executing the bgRFC, but it detects invalid data more easily.

```
  ...
* sRFC to check if data are accepted
CALL FUNCTION 'Z_CREATE_ATHLETE'
DESTINATION pa_dest
  EXPORTING
    i_athlete_name             = lv_name
    i_date_of_birth            = pa_bdate1
```

```
        i_country              = pa_cntry
        i_do_commit            = ' '
    EXCEPTIONS
      missing_authorization    = 1
      invalid_data             = 2
      object_locked            = 3
      OTHERS                   = 4
            .
  IF sy-subrc <> 0.
    WRITE: 'Data not accepted:', sy-subrc.
    EXIT.
  ELSE.
  ...
  * bgRFC for data creation
    CALL FUNCTION 'Z_CREATE_ATHLETE'
      IN BACKGROUND UNIT go_trfc_unit
      EXPORTING
        i_athlete_name         = lv_name
        i_date_of_birth        = pa_bdate1
        i_country              = pa_cntry
        i_do_commit            = ' '
  ...
    COMMIT WORK.
  ENDIF.
```

Listing 1.21: sRFC data check prior to bgRFC call

Another question: how do you create two athletes in one LUW? Can you simply duplicate the bgRFC calls and have one COMMIT WORK statement at the end, just like before for the sRFC? Yes, but you must first decide whether the two athletes should belong to the same LUW.

If you want to put both athletes into one LUW, you use the same unit go_unit for both calls. Otherwise, you create one unit for each call, as depicted in Listing 1.22:

```
gv_dest =
cl_bgrfc_destination_outbound=>create( pa_dest ).
go_unit = gv_dest->create_trfc_unit( ).
```

```
CALL FUNCTION 'Z_CREATE_ATHLETE'
  IN BACKGROUND UNIT go_unit
    EXPORTING
      i_athlete_name                = lv_name1
      i_date_of_birth               = pa_bdate
      i_country                     = pa_cntry
    .
    ...
* This creates a separate unit for the second call
* and decouples the two athletes:
go_unit2 = gv_dest->create_trfc_unit( ).

CALL FUNCTION 'Z_CREATE_ATHLETE'
  IN BACKGROUND UNIT go_unit2
    EXPORTING
      i_athlete_name                = lv_name2
      i_date_of_birth               = pa_bdate
      i_country                     = pa_cntry
    .
    ...
COMMIT WORK.
```

Listing 1.22: Two bgRFC calls in the same or different units

Is a queue required to determine the sequence in which the athletes are created? (That would require a bgRFC with units of the type qRFC.) If both athletes belong to the same LUW, we do not need a queue, as the sequence inside an LUW is retained. But if you decide to have two separate units, the sequence is not guaranteed and you can consider creating a queue in which the sequence is guaranteed. This is not typically required for our example case, the creation of athletes.

1.23 Discussing external numbering

In our scenario, the target system determines the ID for a new athlete using an internal number range. Alternatively, you can use external numbering, in which the client application provides the number.

This scenario has several implications. First, the server must check whether the external number has already been assigned and respond with a respective error message if it has. This does not require a lot of implementation.

The disadvantage of such an approach is that the client application needs to know the format of the athlete number and cannot be sure that a given number will be accepted by the server. On the other hand, as discussed in the last section, a synchronous call (without a COMMIT WORK statement), as shown in the first part of Listing 1.21, can provide the check.

The advantage of external numbering is that when an athlete is created successfully, the client application already knows the athlete ID. In our case, with internal numbering, the client only knows that the data has been stored.

We can extend this discussion to the aspect of exactly-once processing, revealing details about the bgRFC technique used behind the scenes by the ABAP runtime.

To ensure exactly-once processing, the client ABAP runtime creates a *transaction ID* for the bgRFC dataset. This transaction ID is used for the call; if the connection is lost, the same dataset is transmitted with the same transaction ID again. The server ABAP runtime ensures that the dataset for one transaction ID is stored only once, even if it is transmitted several times.

You may be thinking about using an sRFC with external numbering instead of a bgRFC. If the connection is lost, you would simply send the same data (with the same athlete ID) again. If the first call has already created the athlete, the second call would fail and provide the information that the athlete was already created by the first call.

But remember that this implementation requires effort for error handling (handling the status of your athlete data) to resend it if connection errors occur. Moreover, this only covers one part of exactly-once processing: the retry in the case of errors. The other important aspect of asynchronous exactly-once processing is that the client and server applications are decoupled. If you use a bgRFC, your application does not have to wait until the data is successfully stored on the server as the execution is handled by the ABAP runtime. And the ABAP runtime provides monitoring transactions such as SBGRFCMON out of the box.

1.24 Using tRFC and qRFC

Both transactional RFC (tRFC) and queued RFC (qRFC) are predecessors of bgRFC but their use is no longer recommended for new applications. We will take a brief look at the tRFC and qRFC syntax so that you are able to analyze existing coding if necessary.

As you can imagine from the naming, tRFC is equivalent to exactly once (bgRFC with tRFC unit) and qRFC is equivalent to exactly-once-in-order (bgRFC with qRFC unit).

tRFC syntax

The CALL FUNCTION statement is extended by IN BACKGROUND TASK and closed with an explicit COMMIT WORK statement, just like for a bgRFC, as illustrated in Listing 1.23:

```
CALL FUNCTION 'Z_CREATE_ATHLETE'
  IN BACKGROUND TASK
    EXPORTING
    i_athlete_name           = lv_name
    i_date_of_birth          = pa_bdate
    i_country                = pa_cntry
  .
  ...
COMMIT WORK.
```

Listing 1.23: tRFC syntax

You monitor the tRFC calls using transaction SM58 (for bgRFC, we used transaction SBGRFCMON).

SAP delivers the program RSTRFCTI which you can use to create tRFC test calls. You can also use program RSTRFCTI to analyze the coding to learn more about tRFC.

qRFC syntax

The qRFC precedes the CALL FUNCTION statement with the definition of the queue to be used for the subsequent call. Therefore, you provide the queue name to the module TRFC_SET_QUEUE_NAME in a local call, see Listing 1.24:

```
DATA Q_NAME LIKE TRFCQOUT-QNAME.
Q_NAME = 'TEST_QUEUE'.
CALL FUNCTION 'TRFC_SET_QUEUE_NAME'
  EXPORTING
    QNAME = Q_NAME.
CALL FUNCTION 'Z_CREATE_ATHLETE'
IN BACKGROUND TASK
DESTINATION pa_dest
...
COMMIT WORK.
```

Listing 1.24: qRFC syntax

Queues for qRFC are monitored in transaction SMQ2 (outbound queues) and SMQ1 (inbound queues).

SAP delivers the program RSTRFCT0 which you can use to create test qRFC calls. You can also use program RSTRFCT0 to analyze the coding to learn more about qRFC.

1.25 Changing and extending RFMs

Changing the source code of RFMs delivered by SAP as a modification is not recommended. You should always use the Modification Assistant so that your changes can be adapted if SAP delivers a patch for the module.

Another possibility is to consider creating a custom wrapper RFM. You define the interface for this wrapper RFM according to your requirements. In the source code, you implement a local call to the original RFM.

> ### Using a wrapper RFM
>
> A common example is that the original RFM requires an external `COMMIT WORK` statement but your scenario may not allow you to send a subsequent call for this. You create a wrapper RFM, in which you bundle the function call with the necessary `COMMIT WORK` statement in one module.

Some RFMs have a built-in capability to be extended. This approach requires consideration of two aspects:

- ▶ you need a way to pass additional parameters to the RFM,
- ▶ you need the facility to extend the coding with your statements to process your additional parameters.

To allow you to pass additional parameters to the RFM, the interface has extension parameters for importing and exporting data. For the definition of custom coding, the RFM contains a *BAdI (Business Add-In)* for which your implementation class can hold your additional statements. We will see an example of this later in Chapter 2.

When adapting the interface, you have to consider the potential impact on the performance. See Section 1.29 for details.

1.26 Versioning an RFM

Imagine that you have developed, tested, and released your RFM. It will now be used in scenarios and the client applications rely on the existing interface. Changing the RFM interface in an incompatible way would break the scenarios.

Adding additional optional parameters to the interface of an existing RFM is a compatible extension method, as the client applications do not have to adapt their coding. However, if you have requirements to do an incompatible change to the interface of your RFM, you can consider versioning your RFM.

The concept of versioning an interface is based on the idea that several versions of the RFM may coexist, although their interfaces are different.

SAP does not provide a general concept for versioning RFMs in ABAP. Of course, as an RFM is an ABAP object, you can use the general versioning (UTILITIES • VERSIONS • VERSION MANAGEMENT) but this does not allow you to have two versions coexisting. This versioning is also not visible externally.

For a requirement to change the interface in an incompatible way, you have to create a second RFM. This is the only way you can adapt the existing scenarios to the new RFM interface step by step. It is common practice to add a numbering suffix to the name of the RFMs.

1.27 Using non-ABAP RFMs

By definition, RFMs are remote-enabled function modules in ABAP. However, the RFC protocol is supported for non-ABAP systems as well. Therefore, such external systems can use the RFC and this applies to both directions. External client applications can execute an RFM in ABAP and external server applications can provide functionality like an RFM.

The external program has to use the SAP NetWeaver RFC library, or any other of the SAP connectors introduced in Chapter 4. The implementation of such non-ABAP RFMs is not the focus in this book but it is well documented in the SAP NetWeaver RFC library development guide.

Nevertheless, you want to know how to call such an external RFM. The implementation of your client application is as usual: CALL FUNCTION statement with the addition DESTINATION. The relevant part is the RFC destination: it must point to the external server application. And the interface of the non-ABAP RFM is relevant as well. The next section will provide hints for both aspects.

Example report SRFCEXEC

 Look at the example report SRFCEXEC that is delivered by SAP. It tries to call the RFM RFC_REMOTE_EXEC that is delivered with the example executable RFCEXEC as part of the SAP NetWeaver RFC library (see Section 4.1). However, it only works if you have maintained an appropriate RFC destination.

1.28 Creating RFC destinations to non-ABAP

Use transaction SM59 and create a new destination (use upper case letters). Choose type *T (TCP/IP)*. Enter a short text and press Enter. You now have four options for the destination to point to:

1. An external program residing on the application server

2. An external program residing on any remote host

3. An external program residing on the front-end

4. An external program already running as a process

The first three choices are straightforward: specify the host, path and the name of the program. Once such destinations are used, the ABAP runtime will start the external program so that it can handle the call, return the result, and exit.

Figure 1.53 shows the maintenance of the RFC destination of type *T*. In the ACTIVATION TYPE area, REGISTERED SERVER PROGRAM is already selected.

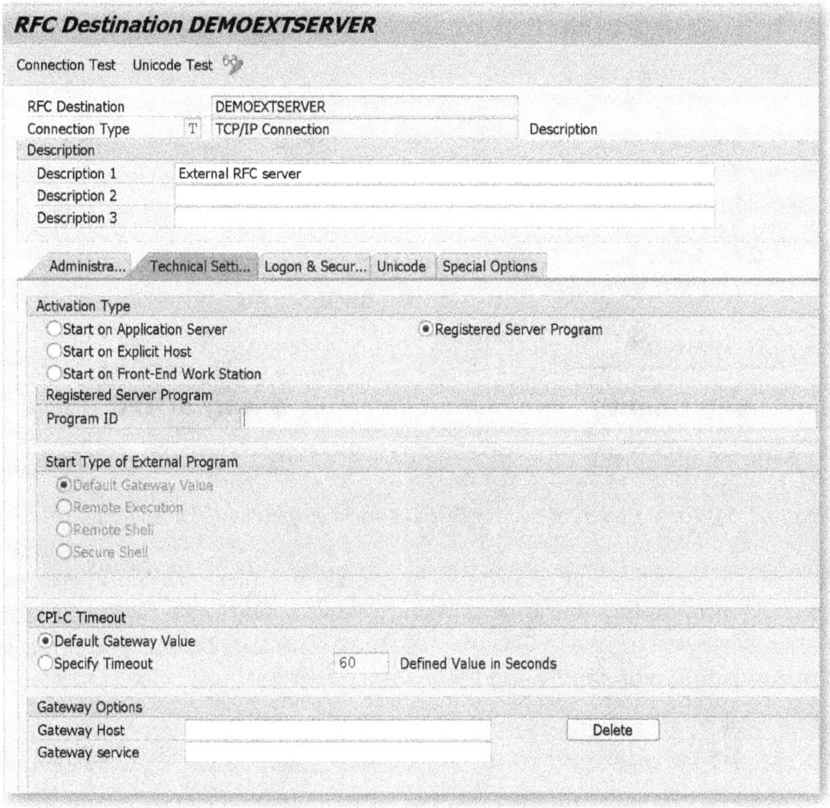

RFC Destination DEMOEXTSERVER

Connection Test   Unicode Test

| RFC Destination | | DEMOEXTSERVER | |
| Connection Type | T | TCP/IP Connection | Description |

Description

Description 1	External RFC server
Description 2	
Description 3	

Administra... Technical Setti... Logon & Secur... Unicode Special Options

Activation Type
- ○ Start on Application Server   ● Registered Server Program
- ○ Start on Explicit Host
- ○ Start on Front-End Work Station

Registered Server Program
Program ID

Start Type of External Program
- ● Default Gateway Value
- ○ Remote Execution
- ○ Remote Shell
- ○ Secure Shell

CPI-C Timeout
- ● Default Gateway Value
- ○ Specify Timeout   60   Defined Value in Seconds

Gateway Options

| Gateway Host | | Delete |
| Gateway service | | |

Figure 1.53: RFC destination type T with gateway registration

The option with registration is different and it is the more realistic one: the external program is an ongoing process that reacts immediately to the call. For the communication to work, the external program must register at a gateway process of an application server of the SAP system using a *program ID*. An example is fax software that is to receive data from the ABAP server.

In turn, the destination must point to this registered program ID at the specific gateway, as depicted in Figure 1.54.

113

Registration of External RFC Server

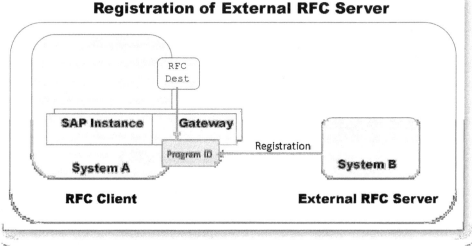

Figure 1.54: Registration of external RFC server at gateway

In the RFC destination, you have to specify the program ID as well as the two parameters for the gateway (section GATEWAY OPTIONS): the fields GATEWAY HOST and GATEWAY SERVICE. The service that you enter is the combination of *sapgw* and the instance number.

Registration is gateway-specific

 One common cause of communication issues is that the registration takes place at one specific gateway. Typically, your SAP system is based on several application servers (instances) and each instance has its own gateway. If you do not maintain the gateway in the destination, the ABAP runtime will try to find the registration on the gateway that belongs to the instance on which the work process is being executed. This may be a different one.

Some external programs can register at several gateways to overcome this trap.

Now that the external RFC server is registered, we can query it on the RFMs provided. In the RFC destination, select EXTRAS • FUNCTION LIST. Depending on the implementation of the external RFC server, a list of the functions provided should appear.

Monitoring registered programs at the gateway

Use the Gateway Monitor (transaction SMGW) and choose GOTO • LOGGED ON CLIENTS. The data displayed will include the program ID.

1.29 Linking serialization and performance

Serialization is the way that a transfer protocol puts the transmitted data to the wire between the client and server system. This potentially includes compression of data. For RFC, several serialization techniques are now available and we will look at and compare them in this section.

In general, the serialization techniques use different compressions. The stronger the compression, the smaller the data size to be transmitted—and the better the performance of an RFC call. This means that the performance of a remote call depends on the serialization used.

Compression considerations

Compressing data takes time, and this must be taken into account as well. For wide-area connections (WAN), the compression time can be neglected. But for local area connections (LAN), a balance between good and fast compression is relevant. In any case, the data transfer performance is related to the serialization technique.

In addition to compression, we have to consider the case that the interfaces of the client and server may differ slightly. Imagine that for the RFM, a parameter was adapted to use a different data type but the RFC client application uses the old version of the interface. For such cases (which are not recommended), the serialization used has a huge impact on the runtime behavior of the RFC.

We will explain how the different RFC serialization techniques are agnostic or repelling to the use of deviant interfaces:

▶ If a data type of a field differs in the client and server: will the field content be transferred if this works without data loss?

▶ If the type difference leads to data loss (example: field length incompatibility): will the user be notified by an exception?

And just to repeat what we already know about performance: the TABLES section in an RFM allows the system to transfer only the delta in the response of a synchronous RFC, instead of the complete table (see Section 1.11).

Transfer protocol

We have already touched on the transfer protocol options briefly, in Section 1.14. Figure 1.35 there showed the required choice of the transfer protocol to enable bgRFC for an RFC destination. The option is displayed in the RFC destination on the SPECIAL OPTIONS tab.

Figure 1.55 now shows all possible options for the transfer protocol. The availability of these options depends on the SAP_BASIS version of your system, as mentioned in the respective explanations below.

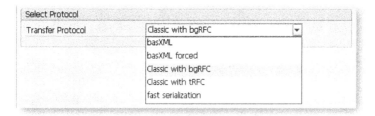

Figure 1.55: Transfer protocol options in the RFC destination

Term: "Transfer protocol"

 Figure 1.55 highlights the parameter TRANSFER PROTOCOL with its possible values. Actually, the options available are not a choice of protocols but rather a mix of queuing techniques (such as bgRFC or tRFC) and serialization techniques (such as basXML or fast serialization). This will be adapted by SAP so that two separate options are provided in the RFC destination. Later, Figure 1.58 will show a preview of this.

We will now discuss the serialization options step by step.

Introducing XRFC

The performance of the RFC protocol depends on whether the transmitted variables have a fixed length or a variable length like a string. For variables with a defined (fixed) length, the *classic RFC* works with *position orientation* such as, for example, that the second data field begins after 6 bytes. This means that there are no tags or positioning markers in the data stream.

However, when strings are transferred, position orientation without markers does not work. A string does not have a fixed length, so a marker is required to flag the end of the actual string value. Therefore, the system then switches to *XRFC*.

XRFC is based on XML and thus allows data marking using the start and end tag for a field. This allows the end of a string field to be flagged.

Further on, XRFC is also used if tables are transferred via the IMPORTING or EXPORTING section of an RFM (instead of the TABLES section) and if structures with deep data types are used.

XRFC

 XRFC was formerly known as RFC-XML. Note that you cannot switch on XRFC explicitly as a data format and you cannot see that this format is used. Figure 1.55 does not show XRFC as an option because the ABAP runtime decides whether it is used (in the case of the two *Classic* options).

However, XRFC does not allow compression of data, which is a performance drawback.

So, let's see what you as a developer of an RFM can do to positively influence the performance of your RFC communication. To avoid an implicit switch to the slower transmission via XRFC serialization, you should:

▶ For table parameters, use the `TABLES` section of an RFM

▶ Avoid adding string parameters to existing RFM interfaces

▶ Avoid structures with deep data types in the RFM interface

Deep data types

 A deep data type contains a reference to another place in the memory. Examples are internal tables, strings, Xstrings.

Introducing basXML

With SAP_BASIS release 7.02, SAP introduced a serialization called *binary ABAP serialization XML (basXML)*. basXML is an SAP-specific format for storing XML files in a binary format, based on UTF-8 as the character encoding standard. It allows compression of all parameters and suppression of redundant information. This is a clear performance advantage compared to classical RFC and XRFC.

basXML: Explicit enablement

 Binary ABAP serialization XML (basXML) can (and must) be explicitly enabled and configured, both on the server side (RFM) and the client side (RFC destination), as discussed below.

Furthermore, it can only be used if the RFM also exists identically in the client system. Only then is the client system aware that the RFM is basXML-enabled.

So how do we enable basXML? The first step is to enable the RFM for basXML, on the ATTRIBUTES tab, see Figure 1.56.

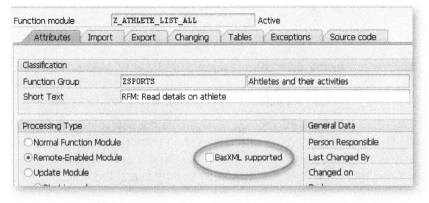

Figure 1.56: BasXML enablement in the attributes of an RFM

The checkbox BASXML SUPPORTED indicates that the use of the module can be based on name identification instead of position identification. Note that this option is only available for remote-enabled modules because all serializations discussed are only relevant for RFC scenarios.

Position identification in classic RFC

 For the classic RFC (without XRFC), if the client provides a variable with the wrong name but with the same position and with the same length as the parameter expected by the RFM, the value will nevertheless be used by the RFM. This is because for classic RFC, the variables are identified by their position, not by their name. However, the use of different variable names is not recommended.

Instead, you should enable basXML when you create RFMs to benefit from the performance advantage of this serialization. Remember that basXML cannot transfer the content of a field if field names differ between the client and server.

If the RFM is basXML-enabled, this serialization is generally possible. To use it, you must enable it on the client side as well. You configure this in the RFC destination, on the SPECIAL OPTIONS tab, as shown in Figure 1.55 above.

basXML requires data type compliance

 All parameters provided in the RFC request must adhere to the data type declarations of the RFM interface. For an RFC using basXML, the RFC transmission is interrupted if a value does not fit the expected data type.

In the RFC request, you should not use values which do not fit the data type defined in the RFM interface. However, sometimes you cannot rely on strict adherence to the expected data type. In these cases, SAP does not recommend the use of basXML.

What about *basXML forced*? Remember that to call an RFM in a remote system, **in general**, the RFM does not have to exist in the client system. But for basXML specifically, it is indeed a requirement that the RFM exists in the client system.

If the RFM does not exist in the client (or it does exist but does not have the BASXML SUPPORTED checkbox enabled), you can nevertheless enforce the use of basXML in the RFC destination by choosing the serialization option basXML forced.

To the list of developer recommendations, we can now add:

▶ You should use basXML when possible, as it allows data compression and improves performance

Interface Check

 As discussed before, the various serialization techniques handle deviations between the interface of the client and server interface differently: basXML, for example, will throw an error for a wrong field name or for a wrong data type.

We call this the type of interface check of the respective serialization.

Introducing fast serialization

Fast serialization was introduced with SAP_BASIS 7.51 and it will be enabled in lower releases (*downported*) as well.

The focus of fast serialization is to drastically improve the RFC performance by means of a higher data compression rate and better performance of data transmission. The design of the fast serialization prioritizes performance improvements and it is based on minimization of round trips, minimal protocol overhead, and the use of different compression algorithms for WAN and LAN scenarios.

Fast serialization and fast RFC

Do not confuse fast serialization with *fast RFC*. Fast RFC is an extension to the RFC library to speed up the communication between ABAP and the java stack for a dual-stack system. It uses shared memory and is only available if the RFC client and RFC server are located on the same host.

Fast serialization is fully compatible with the previous serialization techniques concerning the *interface check*. To ensure this compatibility, if you switch an existing scenario to fast serialization, you must specify which serialization was used previously (this is discussed in more detail below).

Fast serialization has no impact on how you declare and use RFM parameters and on the RFC statement itself in client programs. Furthermore, you do not have to explicitly enable your RFM for fast serialization. You enable fast serialization in the configuration, as discussed in the following section.

The advantage of fast serialization

The advantage of fast serialization is that it allows high performance equally for all data types (fixed or variable length) and even for structures with deep data types. This makes the development of new and the enhancement of existing RFM interfaces easy, even without complex expert knowledge.

Enabling fast serialization

If the client system supports fast serialization (which depends only on the SAP_BASIS release version), you can activate this serialization in the RFC destination in the client system, as shown in Figure 1.55 above. Fast serialization only works if the server system supports fast serialization as well. (You can check this using the test explained below.)

An RFC destination on a release that supports fast serialization shows an additional button FAST SERIALIZATION TEST, as highlighted in Figure 1.57. Note that you should run the test when you have opened the RFC destination in edit mode, otherwise it will only show reduced information.

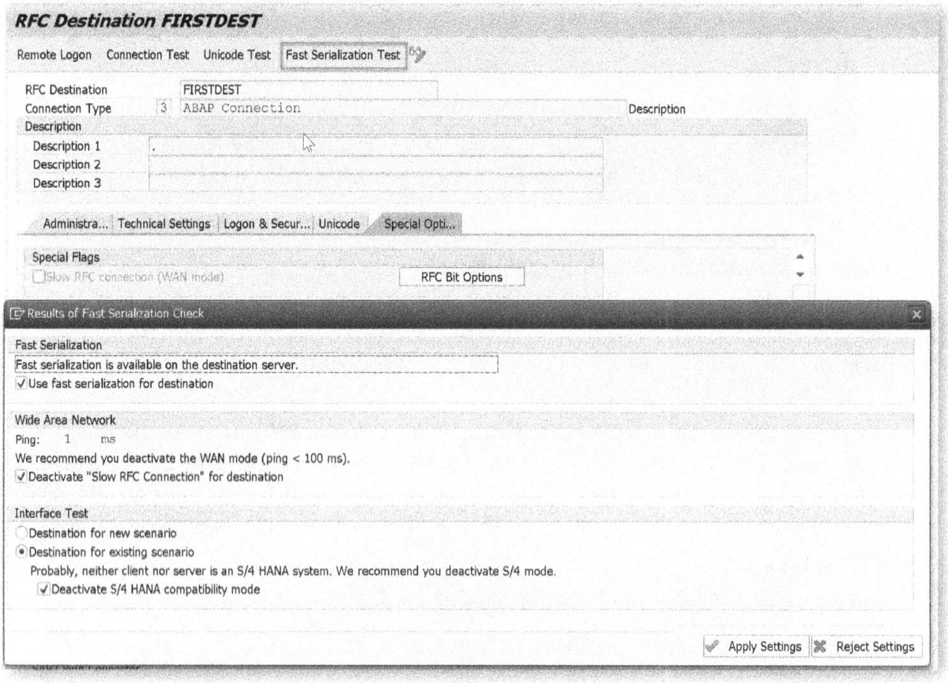

Figure 1.57: Fast serialization test in RFC destination

This test reveals several aspects:

▶ It checks whether the **target** supports fast serialization as well

▶ It proposes how you should set the option SLOW RFC CONNECTION (WAN MODE) because fast serialization uses different compression algorithms for WAN and LAN scenarios

▶ In the case of an existing destination, it proposes the following choices for the section interface check:

   ▶ The compatibility choice
   ▶ The SAP S/4HANA-related option
   (both are explained in the next section)

Interface check for fast serialization

If fast serialization is not only possible but also chosen, the RFC destination shows the additional section INTERFACE CHECK FOR FAST SERIALIZATION on the SPECIAL OPTIONS tab, below the serialization choice, see Figure 1.58.

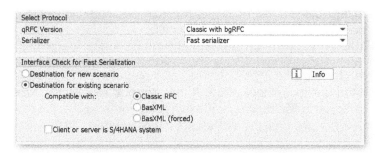

Figure 1.58: Type of interface check for fast serialization

Note that the upper part of Figure 1.58 already shows the new approach, offering two separate options (queueing and serialization) instead of one option TRANSFER PROTOCOL.

123

Let's start with the simple case. If you choose the option DESTINATION FOR NEW SCENARIO, the compatibility options are not shown, as they are not relevant. Choose this option if you are implementing a new scenario and thus creating a new RFC destination (instead of switching an existing RFC destination to fast serialization).

In contrast, if you have used the destination before and now want to switch to fast serialization, you can keep the behavior of the system compatible to the previous behavior (with regard to the interface check). In this case, choose the option DESTINATION FOR EXISTING SCENARIO and specify which serialization was used before.

Migrating an existing destination to fast serialization

If you want to change an existing RFC destination to use fast serialization, select FAST SERIALIZATION TEST **before** you switch the protocol. This means that the test will propose the compatibility choice based on the previous serialization.

If you instead first switch the serialization to fast serialization and then execute the test, the test can no longer propose the appropriate compatibility choice. You will have to set it manually.

The interface check of the ABAP runtime will then behave in the same way as with the previous serialization. If the previous serialization was tolerant to particular types of structure extensions, for example, the fast serialization will behave similarly and will not throw an error.

Another aspect for the case DESTINATION FOR EXISTING SCENARIO is that you must specify whether one of the systems involved is an SAP S/4HANA system (client or server). This is relevant because some interfaces may have changed in SAP S/4HANA compared to SAP ERP. See Section 5.2 for details on this point.

When you use the fast serialization test in the RFC destination (see Figure 1.57 above), the system checks whether the client or server are SAP S/4HANA systems and proposes how you should set the option CLIENT OR SERVER IS S/4HANA SYSTEM.

Finally, we can now add the following recommendation:

▶ Use fast serialization whenever possible as it offers the highest level of performance without the need for expert knowledge

The requirement is that both the client and server support fast serialization. SAP is working on a downport of fast serialization to lower SAP_BASIS releases as well, even down to SAP_BASIS 7.00.

We have now reached our first milestone on the journey through interface technologies. We started with the protocol RFC and RFMs as interfaces and we have discussed testing and error handling. We examined the aspect of synchronous and asynchronous interfaces which are relevant for other interface technologies as well.

Let us now take the next step to BAPIs: a technology with similar aspects.

2 Using BAPIs

If you ask experienced colleagues what a BAPI is, their answers may range from "Oh, just another RFM" to "A method to access business data inside SAP solutions encapsulated in a business object". Both statements are correct: the colleagues just see things from different angles. We will start by looking at the shorter answer: a BAPI is a remote-enabled function module.

2.1 Calling a BAPI by RFC in three minutes

A BAPI is an RFM and its name starts with BAPI_. If, for example, you want to get a list of users from the target system, your coding may look as shown in Listing 2.1:

```
REPORT  z_bapi_call.
PARAMETERS pa_dest
        TYPE rfcdes-rfcdest DEFAULT 'FIRSTDEST'.
DATA: t_user TYPE TABLE OF bapiusname,
      l_user TYPE bapiusname.

CALL FUNCTION 'BAPI_USER_GETLIST'
  DESTINATION pa_dest
  TABLES
    userlist = t_user.

LOOP AT t_user INTO l_user.
  WRITE: /, l_user-username.
ENDLOOP.
```

Listing 2.1: Simplified RFC to BAPI example

Was that all we need to know about BAPIs? Of course not ... and again this introductory coding is not sufficient, so let us dig deeper.

2.2 Getting the overview on BAPIs

With the knowledge from the previous chapter on RFCs, you can already call a BAPI using RFC as the protocol, as the BAPI implementation is always an RFM. So why are you reading this chapter? BAPIs offer some very important and helpful features for your remote communication but also hold some traps—so it is worth examining some of the details. You may also be curious about what "BAPI implementation" means.

Let's start with the name: *BAPI* is the abbreviation for *Business API*, in the sense of an interface to business data.

BAPI or BAdI

 Do not confuse a BAPI with a BAdI: a *BAdI* is a *Business Add-In* for a modification-free extension of existing ABAP coding. And a BAPI may offer a BAdI—a point to extend the BAPI without modification, as we will discuss later.

If an RFM implements a BAPI, then you know how to examine the BAPI: you examine the RFM. Nevertheless, if the RFM is the **implementation**, there must be something beyond the implementation, some meta level that the RFM is implementing.

You can use the Function Builder selection screen to search for RFMs with the prefix BAPI_. (In Section 2.3, we will discuss a smarter way to search for BAPIs.) The next part of the name is the object to which the BAPI is related. Remember: the other colleague mentioned something like "data … encapsulated in a business object".

The "object" belongs to the meta level beyond the implementation. This object is a representation of business data to which the BAPI shall offer an interface. A simple example is BAPI_USER_GETLIST: this BAPI provides a list of system users, so **User** is the object type to work on and **getlist** is the method—makes sense, doesn't it? Figure 2.1 illustrates the business object with its methods and the related RFMs which are relevant for the RFC communication.

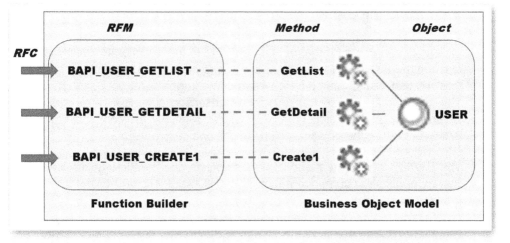

Figure 2.1: Relationship between the business object, method, and RFM

Open this BAPI (the RFM BAPI_USER_GETLIST) in the Function Builder and check the attributes: the function module is indeed remote-enabled. However, if you are looking for attributes revealing that this RFM is a BAPI, there is no clue available here, the only indication is the name.

Moreover, the source code of the BAPI-RFM is just like the source code for any other RFM. Therefore, we need another way to examine BAPIs and find out what makes them special.

Object-oriented technique or module technique

 Although a BAPI relates to an object, the coding is not **object-oriented** in the sense that the object belongs to an ABAP class. No ABAP class exists for the object to which the BAPI belongs.

Nevertheless, the implementation inside the function module can use ABAP object statements, just like any other RFM implementation.

2.3 Exploring BAPIs

Instead of searching for the name of an RFM in the Function Builder, you can use the *BAPI Explorer*. This is a comfortable and well-structured tool that you can use to search for an appropriate interface for your scenario. You open the BAPI Explorer using the transaction code BAPI—it's easy to remember. Nevertheless, the BAPI Explorer initially does not show the BAPIs but rather the objects, which we call *business objects*.

The BAPI Explorer lists these business objects and their interfaces (BAPIs) by application component hierarchy (HIERARCHICAL tab) or by name (ALPHABETICAL tab).

BAPI benefit: Easy to find

 You can find appropriate BAPIs for your project in the BAPI Explorer using the application component hierarchy for orientation.

Switch to the ALPHABETICAL tab first and then scroll down to select the object *USER*. The DETAIL tab then displays details for this object, as shown in Figure 2.2.

The right-hand side of the screen offers additional tabs: DOCUMENTATION indicates that each business object, with its BAPIs, is well documented; the PROJECT tab offers a guided way to create your own business objects and BAPIs; the TOOLS tab offers several tools based on the object selected.

BAPI benefit: Well documented

 You will find documentation for each BAPI. This is in contrast to RFMs, which may not be documented by SAP in each case.

Now select the method *GetList* of the object *USER*. The details reveal the name of the RFM that implements the BAPI, as shown in Figure 2.3.

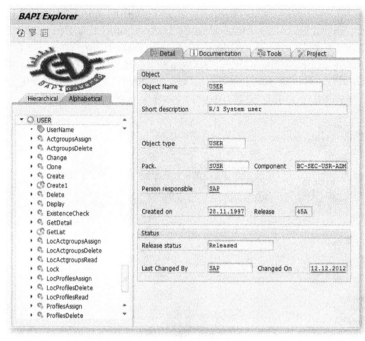

Figure 2.2: Transaction BAPI shows details for the object USER

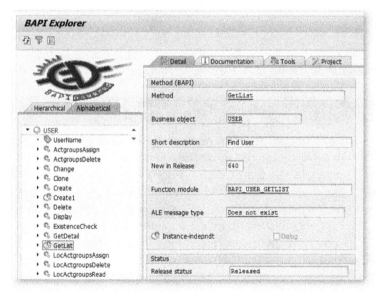

Figure 2.3: Details for BAPI_USER_GETLIST

Double-clicking the name of the function module would open the RFM in the Function Builder. As we have already investigated the RFM in the Function Builder, instead, select the TOOLS tab, then in the TOOL SELECTION section, select FUNCTION BUILDER. You will see the familiar buttons from the Function Builder for displaying, changing, or executing a single test for the function module, as shown in Figure 2.4.

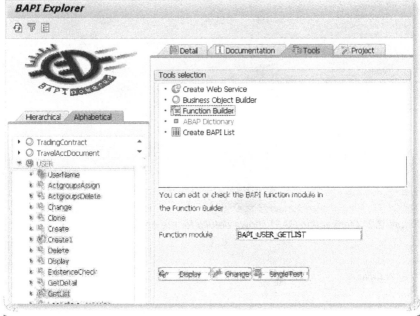

Figure 2.4: Tools section in the BAPI Explorer

Business objects and business object types

 Following an accurate nomenclature, we should say that the BAPI Explorer shows the business object **types**, for example the type USER. It does not show the **object** like the user ADMIN. A business object **type** defines the attributes and methods for each business **object** at meta level. Business objects are manifest implementations of the business object type. They have concrete values for the possible attributes, such as User Name = ADMIN. This is in accordance with object orientation. The business object type correlates to the class, the business object relates to the object.

However, let us return to the DETAIL view of the BAPI, as shown in Figure 2.3. Most of this information is self-explanatory. Let us pick out the icon and the attribute INSTANCE-INDEPNDT. Choose GOTO • DISPLAY LEGEND to check the legend, which is shown in Figure 2.5.

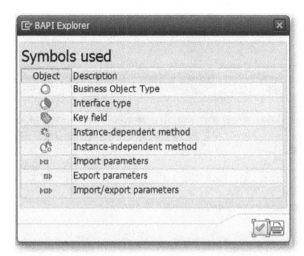

Figure 2.5: Legend for icons in the BAPI Explorer

For instance-dependent methods, you have to provide the key fields to specify the object instance you want to work on. Check this out for the BAPIs GetList and GetDetail: the key field is UserName. Of course, it makes sense to provide the name for a user to get the details listed; in contrast, it does not make sense to specify a user name to get a list of users.

If you now investigate the interface parameters of the BAPI GetDetail, you will not find the key field UserName listed in the BAPI Explorer. In the BAPI Explorer, you must know that key fields are import parameters of instance-dependent BAPIs. Nevertheless, the Function Builder will reveal that the function module BAPI_USER_GETDETAIL has an import parameter USERNAME. Figure 2.6 compares the interface display for a BAPI in the BAPI Explorer and in the Function Builder.

If you examine the other import parameters listed in the BAPI Explorer for *GetDetail* (shown in Figure 2.6 on the left-hand side), you will see *ExtIDPart* and *ExtIDHead* listed as import parameters. In the Function Builder, they are included on the TABLES tab.

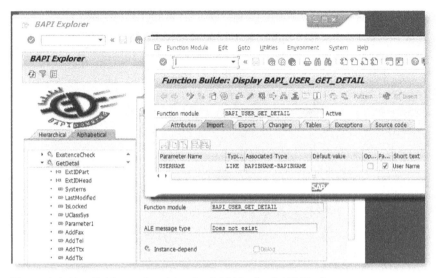

Figure 2.6: Key fields not listed for the BAPI in the BAPI Explorer

BAPI benefit: More specific interface information

 The BAPI Explorer shows the intended data flow (import or export) for TABLES parameters of a function module. This information is missing in the Function Builder, as technically you can use TABLES parameters for import and/or export. So, for a plain RFM, you do not know whether data provided to the TABLES section by the client is used by the RFM coding or not.

While we are comparing the interface representation of RFMs in the Function Builder with the BAPI Explorer display: how about exceptions? Indeed, BAPIs do not use the exception concept!

BAPI benefit: Easy access from external systems

 BAPIs offer access to business data inside SAP and they omit exceptions to ease the access from non-ABAP systems.

No RFM that represents a BAPI uses the exceptions part of the interface. Instead, each BAPI offers an export parameter RETURN that provides information about success or failure during the execution of the function module. The BAPI Explorer lists RETURN as an export parameter; the Function Builder lists this either as an `EXPORT` parameter or as part of the `TABLES` section (for providing several messages), depending on the actual BAPI.

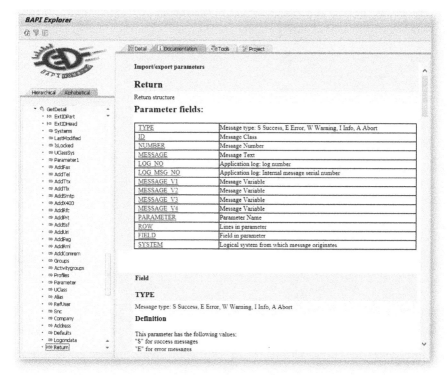

Figure 2.7: BAPI structure RETURN

Checking the RETURN structure for BAPIs

Let's continue our examination of the object USER. Still in the BAPI Explorer, for the BAPI GetDetail, select the parameter *Return* and select the tab DOCUMENTATION. *Return* has a field TYPE as the message type, with possible values *S, E, W, I, A* (see Figure 2.7). Note that some BAPIs leave the field TYPE empty for a successful call, instead of filling it with *S* for success.

Select the BAPI *Create1* and choose the TOOLS tab. Select FUNCTION BUILDER and execute a single test. Enter *noname* as the user name and execute the call. On the results screen, scroll down to the TABLES section to find *RETURN*. Click the icon next to 1 ENTRY to see the error message with the text USER NONAME DOES NOT EXIST.

Let us now extend the very first example on BAPI usage in ABAP (Listing 2.1) to a more comprehensive example report. We will consider the RFC exceptions and evaluate the table parameter RETURN. See Listing 2.2:

```
REPORT   z_bapi_call.

PARAMETERS pa_dest
TYPE rfcdes-rfcdest DEFAULT 'FIRSTDEST'.
DATA: t_user TYPE TABLE OF bapiusname,
      t_return TYPE TABLE OF bapiret2,
      l_return TYPE bapiret2,
      l_user TYPE bapiusname,
      l_error TYPE boolean,
      gv_msg(100).

CALL FUNCTION 'BAPI_USER_GETLIST'
  DESTINATION pa_dest
  TABLES
    userlist              = t_user
    return                = t_return
  EXCEPTIONS
    system_failure        = 1   MESSAGE gv_msg
    communication_failure = 2   MESSAGE gv_msg
  .
CASE sy-subrc.
  WHEN 1 OR 2.
    WRITE: gv_msg.
    EXIT.
ENDCASE.

LOOP AT t_return INTO l_return.
  WRITE: /, l_return-type, l_return-message.
  CASE l_return-type.
```

```
    WHEN '' OR 'S'.
      " table entry is no error
    WHEN OTHERS.
      l_error = abap_true.
  ENDCASE.
ENDLOOP.

IF NOT l_error = abap_true.
  WRITE: 'user list from', pa_dest.
  LOOP AT t_user INTO l_user.
    WRITE: /, l_user-username.
  ENDLOOP.
ENDIF.
```

Listing 2.2: BAPI call considering RFC exceptions and RETURN

Checking RETURN

Listing 2.2 executes a check for a positive result, so for content ' ' or 'S' in the field TYPE. Alternatively, you can check for a negative result, that is, for an error or abort:
`IF l_return-type CA 'EA'.`

If BAPIs do not use exceptions, is there anything else they avoid? Yes: dialogs! An SAP system offers BAPIs as methods for external systems to access business data. BAPIs do not use ABAP user interface technologies like a WRITE statement or a dynpro because external systems cannot handle these.

If you look closely at Figure 2.3, you will see the DIALOG checkbox in the details of the BAPI *GetDetail*. It is obvious that this checkbox only makes sense if there are BAPIs that have the checkbox enabled. This is in fact the case: some BAPIs do use dialog technique! At least they are honest enough to tell you so.

Example of a dialog BAPI: User.Display

 Still in the BAPI Explorer, at our example business object USER: examine the details for BAPI Display: it is one of these exceptions. The DIALOG checkbox is selected and an appropriate icon ⊞ is shown.

These dialog BAPIs are for ABAP-to-ABAP communication only: if the ABAP client system calls a BAPI in a remote system that processes dynpro logic, the session of the client system can display the dynpro.

It is very beneficial to know beforehand whether an RFM uses dialog technique or not. For BAPIs, the BAPI Explorer documents this; non-BAPI RFMs do not offer this information.

BAPI benefit: Dialog-free communication

 Most BAPIs do not use dialogs to enable program-to-program communication. The display of information is up to the client. BAPIs with dialogs are easy to detect and are for ABAP-to-ABAP communication only.

Let's have a look at BAPIs for changing existing objects, such as User.Change. For this type of change, you want to provide only the new data and keep other data at its existing value. For example, you want to adapt the FUNCTION field of the user and you will use the import parameter ADDRESS to do this. This structure contains a lot of fields that you do not want to overwrite—on the other hand, you do not want to provide all existing values. However, if you only provide new values for some fields of the import parameter ADDRESS, the remaining fields will be kept to their default values in the parameter. But how can the BAPI know that you do not want to overwrite the existing values of these fields with the default value? The answer is: you use the X structures!

BAPIs for changing data on an existing object typically offer X structures as a kind of shadow structure. If you want to change a field, you have to fill the respective field of the X structure (with the identical name) with string X to indicate that the field of the original structure should be changed. That way, the BAPI can distinguish, for example, whether the existing field should be overwritten with the default value of a variable or if the field should remain unchanged. Figure 2.8 shows the X structure BAPIADDR3X for BAPI structure BAPIADDR. All fields are typed as CHAR 1, as they can only contain SPACE or X.

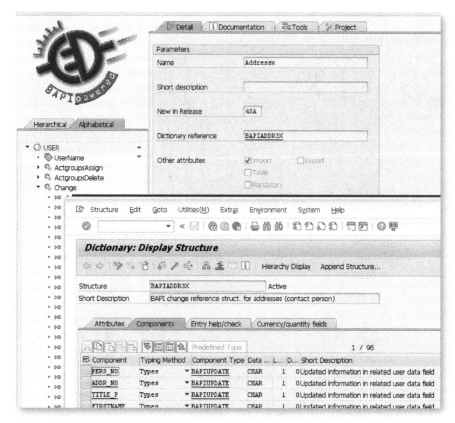

Figure 2.8: X structure BAPIADDR3X with char1 fields

Let us see how this works in another short demo report, as shown in Listing 2.3.

```
REPORT  z_user_change.

DATA: l_username TYPE bapibname-bapibname,

      l_address TYPE bapiaddr3,
      l_addressx TYPE bapiaddr3x,
```

```
      gv_msg(100),
      t_return TYPE TABLE OF bapiret2,
      l_return TYPE bapiret2,
      l_err_mess TYPE bapiret2-message,
      l_error TYPE boolean.

PARAMETERS:
pa_usr(15) DEFAULT 'TESTER',
pa_func TYPE bapiaddr3-title_p DEFAULT 'Director',
pa_dest TYPE rfcdes-rfcdest DEFAULT 'FIRSTDEST'.

l_username = pa_usr.
l_address-function = pa_func.
l_addressx-function = 'X'.

CALL FUNCTION 'BAPI_USER_CHANGE'
  DESTINATION pa_dest
  EXPORTING
    username            = l_username
    address             = l_address
    addressx            = l_addressx
  TABLES
    return              = t_return
  EXCEPTIONS
    system_failure      = 1  MESSAGE gv_msg
    communication_failure = 2  MESSAGE gv_msg.

CASE sy-subrc.
  WHEN 1 OR 2.
    WRITE: sy-subrc, gv_msg.
    EXIT.
ENDCASE.

LOOP AT t_return INTO l_return.
  WRITE: /, l_return-type, l_return-message.
  CASE l_return-type.
    WHEN '' OR 'S'.
      " table entry is no error
    WHEN OTHERS.
      l_error = abap_true.
```

```
      WRITE l_return-message.
   ENDCASE.
ENDLOOP.

IF NOT l_error = abap_true.
   WRITE: 'User data were changed, ', pa_dest.
ENDIF.
```

Listing 2.3: Using X structures for BAPIs with data changes

Another important aspect that plain RFMs do not reveal is how they handle data changes. For BAPIs, this is defined: they use the update technique—but you must be aware of that. A typical hurdle for development projects using BAPIs is that developers involved are not aware of the BAPI concept of the update technique. If the COMMIT WORK statement is missing, no data is stored, as explained in the next paragraph.

Changes to the database using SQL statements require a closing COMMIT WORK statement to close the logical unit of work (LUW). Without this statement, the ABAP runtime will not persist the changes to the database. Imagine you want to store data in the target system, that is, write the data to the target database. If you provide data from your RFC client to an appropriate RFM (which triggers the SQL statements) but the RFM does not include the COMMIT WORK statement, your data is lost the moment that the connection is closed.

Non-BAPI RFMs do not reveal whether they include the COMMIT WORK statement—this information, if it is provided at all, may be included in the documentation. For BAPIs, the development guide states that you should NOT include the COMMIT WORK statement in the BAPI.

In detail: the BAPI uses the statement CALL FUNCTION ... IN UPDATE TASK to write the data to the update tables. The registered update entries are written to the database only when the COMMIT WORK statement is triggered by an explicit call to BAPI_TRANSACTION_COMMIT. We have discussed this approach already, see Figure 1.43. This is now depicted in Figure 2.9.

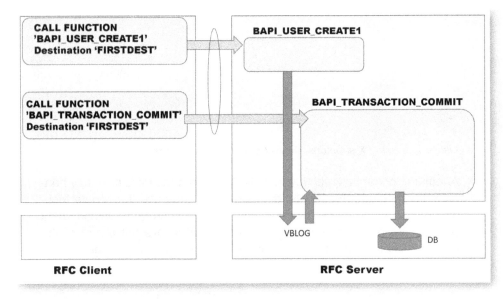

Figure 2.9: External COMMIT WORK statement for BAPI calls

Note that both calls must be done via one RFC connection, that is why the two arrows are bundled with a small circle. Technically, the update table is part of the database as well, so this part of Figure 2.9 is not accurate.

Wait a minute—remember the last coding example, in which we changed the data for an existing user? Where was the external COMMIT WORK statement? If you check the coding, you will see that it was not required: indeed, some BAPIs execute the COMMIT WORK statement on their own. This is true for early BAPIs and a couple of exceptional BAPIs.

Exceptional BAPIs with internal COMMIT WORK statement

 BAPIs were introduced before SAP R/3 4.0. With that release, the development guideline states that the COMMIT WORK statement shall no longer be part of the RFM itself. However, there are earlier BAPIs which are an exception to the rule. SAP Note 131838 lists additional BAPIs.

Why should it be a benefit to require an external COMMIT WORK statement? You can trigger the required COMMIT WORK statement from your client. You can do so by calling the BAPI BAPI_TRANSACTION _COMMIT, as it contains the COMMIT WORK statement, and thus your data is stored. In addition, you can control when to commit the changes. You can execute several calls and finally decide to trigger the commit or not—depending on the overall results. Accordingly, to withdraw the LUW, you use the BAPI BAPI_TRANSACTION_ROLLBACK.

BAPI benefit: Update technique with external commit

BAPIs use the update technique and do not trigger the required COMMIT WORK statement. If you use an existing RFM instead, you have to find out yourself how it handles the update.

BAPIs are the explicit interface to ABAP processes, also for non-ABAP systems. To ease the access, BAPIs offer relevant interface parameters in ISO format in addition to the ABAP internal format.

Checking the return structure ADDRESS for User.GetDetail

The return structure ADDRESS for User.GetDetail references BAPIADDR3. This structure has the field COUNTRY as an ABAP-internal representation (CHAR length 3) and the field COUNTRYISO as an ISO representation (CHAR length 2).

The benefit is that external applications do not have to know the ABAP-internal format and they use the ISO format instead.

BAPI benefit: ISO format offered as external format

BAPIs can be used from external applications with the ISO format instead of the ABAP-internal format.

As explicit interfaces to business data, BAPIs offer a stable interface, even after an upgrade or with a new enhancement package. This means that external client applications do not have to be adapted immediately after such a software change.

> ## BAPI benefit: Stable interface
>
> BAPI interfaces are **frozen** and an update of the SAP software does not lead to incompatible changes in the interface.

However, how does SAP handle incompatible changes in the interface of a BAPI? The versioning concept is easy: SAP introduces another BAPI with a similar name (and a number suffix). New external applications should use the new BAPI and for existing applications, the switch can take place later after the SAP update.

> ## Versioning of BAPIs: Business object USER
>
> In our ongoing example, let us take the BAPIs Create and Create1 of business object type USER as an example: SAP introduced Create1 with SAP R/3 4.6C and marked Create as deprecated. The BAPI Explorer shows a warning icon for this deprecated BAPI.

2.4 Using BAPI services

Another important benefit is that the BAPI usage is supported by some service BAPIs. SAP delivers two rather technical business objects BapiService and HelpValues for this.

The first object, BapiService, provides BAPIs that support you in the conversion between internal and external data format. It also provides meta-information on BAPIs. Check out the BAPI Explorer to find the list of these service BAPIs. We will take one example to start with: BapiService.InterfaceGetDocu. It lists the documentation for an interface.

> ### Testing the BAPI BapiService.InterfaceGetDocu
>
> Select the BAPI in the BAPI Explorer and switch to the TOOLS tab. Select FUNCTION BUILDER and start a single test. Let us execute a recursive action: we reference the BAPI that we are testing. Enable the UPPER-CASE/LOWERCASE checkbox, enter *BapiService* in the OBJNAME field, *InterfaceGetDocu* in the METHOD field, and *HTM* in the TEXTFORMAT field. Execute the test and examine the table TEXT: it lists the documentation for the BAPI.

The object BapiService offers additional BAPIs for switching between the external and internal representation of data, such as the country: DataConversionExt2Int1 and DataConversionInt2Ext1. They take the object and BAPI method as well as the parameter as input and provide a conversion to the other format respectively.

The other object, HelpValues, provides information on help values for BAPI parameters. We will examine this in Section 2.6.

2.5 Extending BAPIs

Imagine that for your scenario, there is no BAPI available that fits your requirements. We have already discussed this case for plain RFMs: you should first check the feasibility of extending an existing BAPI before considering creating your own interface. It is simply less work than creating your own BAPI.

The interface of a BAPI is designed with more restrictions than a plain RFM, so there is even less reason to modify it. And the BAPI development guide allows the modification-free extension of a BAPI—as explained in this section.

The aim of extending a BAPI is to exchange more data between two systems than was originally designed by the specific parameters of the BAPI interface. The BAPI extension concept therefore comprises two aspects:

▶ generic extension parameters in the RFM interface (for additional fields), and

▶ enhancement points in the source code of the RFM (for additional coding).

This is illustrated in Figure 2.10.

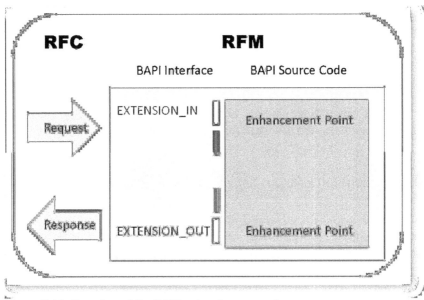

Figure 2.10: Overview of the BAPI extension concept

Classical or new BAdI concept

 The technology in the BAPI source code can be based on the classical BAdI concept (Business Add-In) or on the new enhancement framework which uses *enhancement points*. The approach is the same for both technologies.

The structure of the extension parameters (EXTENSION_IN and EX-
TENSION_OUT) must be generic, as they must fit for diverse customer
fields. During the design of the BAPI (by SAP), the additional fields that
will be used later by customer extensions are not known. It is the customer who defines a specific structure for the additional fields. This structure must then be passed to the BAPI, together with the data, as we will
see in our example later.

The extension parameters EXTENSION_IN and EXTENSION_OUT reference the generic structure BAPIPAREX. This structure contains on the
one hand a field for the name of the structure (with the additional fields),
and on the other hand four fields for the content of the customer fields
(VALUEPART1 … to 4). Therefore, the additional content must deliver a
structure name as a mask to interpret the data (see Figure 2.11).

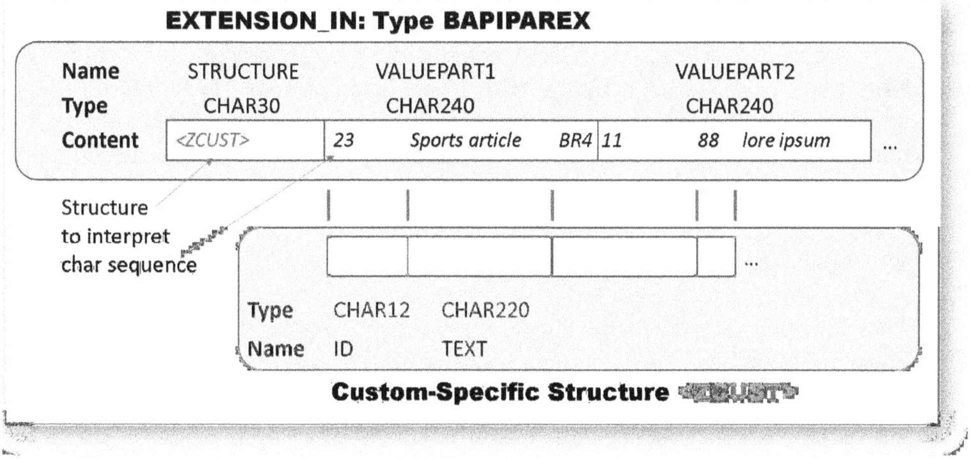

Figure 2.11: Generic structure BAPIPAREX filled with specific data

For this purpose, EXTENSION_IN must hold the structure name (field
STRUCTURE) and the data (fields VALUEPART1 to VALUEPART4). The
structure name is depicted as <ZCUST> in Figure 2.11 above.

Overview of extension scenarios

There are basically three scenarios for using the extension parameters.
The enhancement points in the source code are not required in all cases.
The three scenarios are as follows:

▶ Passing additional selection or filter criteria

- ► Considering additional fields of an SAP table append

- ► Considering additional fields of a customer table

► Passing additional selection or filter criteria

You can provide additional selection or filter information in the parameter EXTENSION_IN to be considered in the processing of the BAPI. The enhancement point in the source code of the BAPI can be used to implement custom coding to check the data provided, if desired. The data provided is not written to the database; it is used only to narrow down the result provided by the BAPI. This scenario is typically used for GetList or GetDetail BAPIs.

► Considering additional fields of an SAP table append

This scenario is based on a table append on the respective SAP database table which is used by the BAPI. The fields provided in the extension parameters have the same structure as the table append. This scenario does not require the use of the enhancement points in the source code. We will elaborate on this scenario in detail below.

► Considering additional fields of a customer table

This scenario is used when the customer has created their own database table and the BAPI should consider this as well. Additional fields are used in the extension parameters and the custom coding implementing the enhancement point can read and/or write to the customer-specific table.

BAPI extension example: Table appends

Let's assume that you have found a BAPI that is almost suitable for your scenario: it takes input (from the RFC request) and writes it into an SAP-defined table. What's missing is that this SAP table has a customer append, and you want the BAPI to consider your additional fields to be written into this table append.

The advantage of this scenario is that you do not have to consider the enhancement points in the source code of the BAPI, so you do not have to implement additional coding. If you follow the rules, your additional fields will be considered by the existing coding of the BAPI. So, what are these rules? The rules describe which structure you use to provide your additional fields and how you embed these into the extension parameter in the BAPI interface.

SAP delivers a structure as a kind of template for structuring your additional fields. Its purpose is to structure the additional data provided via EXTENSION_IN. The structure name is BAPI_TE_<TABLE>, where TE is the abbreviation for table extension. <TABLE> is the name of the table that holds the business object data, the table that was extended with the customer append. The BAPI_TE_<TABLE> structure provided must be extended as well with a customer append in the DDIC to hold the customer-specific fields.

Figure 2.12 illustrates the extension concept.

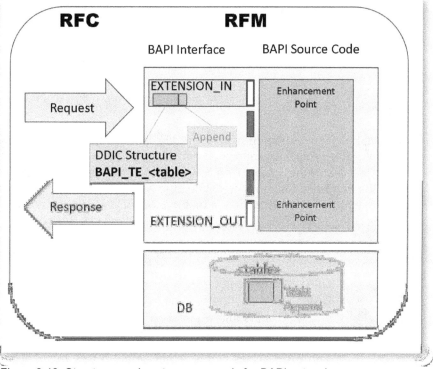

Figure 2.12: Structures and customer appends for BAPI extension

These are the actions required for the preparation phase:

▶ Determine BAPI

▶ Identify database table and associated table extend structure

▶ Create appends for table and structure

These steps are a prerequisite, so they must be done during the design phase. They will allow that during runtime (during the RFC), additional data can be provided via the parameter EXTENSION_IN of the RFC request so that this data is written to the database.

Application BAPI used in the example

 Note that up to this point, we have used functionality in this book that is provided in a plain application server ABAP. This allows you to follow the examples and exercises without the need for a full-blown SAP ECC system. For the following example, we must leave this path, as only the application components (part of SAP ECC) offer BAPIs with the appropriate extension concept.

▶ Determine the BAPI

Let's elaborate on an example from the logistics area. In the hierarchy view of the BAPI Explorer, choose LOGISTICS – GENERAL • LOGISTICS BASIC DATA to find a business object type STANDARDMATERIAL (see Figure 2.13). Check the key field: it is the material number MATNR with CHAR 18 (not shown in figure). The object offers a method, *SaveData*, with the associated RFM *BAPI_MATERIAL_SAVEDATA*. We will extend this BAPI.

BAPI_MATERIAL_SAVEDATA

 Don't get confused: the RFM name BAPI_MATERIAL_ SAVEDATA sounds as if the object name is Material but this RFM is the implementation of the method SaveData for business object type StandardMaterial.

The BAPI allows you to either create a new material or update an existing material.

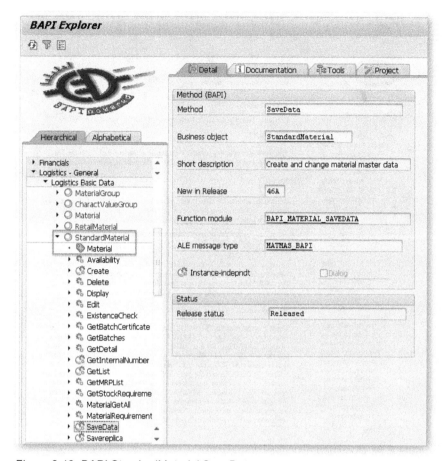

Figure 2.13: BAPI StandardMaterial.SaveData

▶ Identify the database table and associated table extend structure

Check the BAPI documentation in the BAPI Explorer: it mentions (at the end) that the explanation of how to maintain customer-defined fields is to be found in the documentation of parameter EXTENSION_IN. You can compare it with the picture provided above in Figure 2.12. What we skipped in the overview picture are the x structures for database changes.

The documentation for parameter EXTENSION_IN mentions the table extend structures as well as the respective database tables (see Figure 2.14).

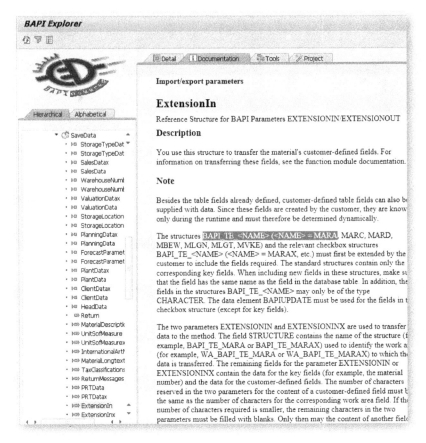

Figure 2.14: Documentation for ExtensionIn

We will choose table MARA. The template for the customer structure is then BAPI_TE_MARA. Therefore, we need a table append for transparent table MARA that holds the additional fields, and another append for structure BAPI_TE_MARA. For simplicity, we will just add one field in each append, using the name ZZSPORTS. Note that the field name must be identical for the table append and the structure append, otherwise the data transfer will not work. If you intend to append several fields, it makes sense to create a structure with these fields and reference this structure, instead of filling all fields manually.

▶ Create appends for table and structure

Use transaction SE11 to start the ABAP Dictionary and then display table MARA. Click APPEND STRUCTURE ... to display a dialog box with the existing appends. In this dialog box, click [icon] CREATE APPEND and specify *ZSPORTS_APP* as the append name in the subsequent dialog box (see Figure 2.15).

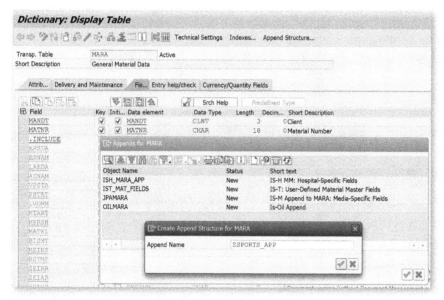

Figure 2.15: Creating a table append for MARA

Confirm with ⌊Enter⌋. The maintenance dialog for the append then appears. Maintain a short text and fill the line for one field with component *ZZSPORTS*, referencing *CHAR 42* (use the button PREDEFINED TYPES if required) (see Figure 2.16).

Append Structure	ZSPORTS_APP	New
Short Description	Table append for MARA	

| Attrib... | Compone... | Entry help/check | Currency/quantity fields |

⬚ Component	Key	Initi...	Typing M...	Co...	Data Type	Length	Decimal Pl	Short Description
ZZSPORTS	☐	☐	Types ▼		CHAR	42	0	Sports related material information

Figure 2.16: Maintaining table append for MARA

Check and activate the append. You can choose SHOW APPENDING OBJ (see Figure 2.16) to get the field list for table MARA with all appended fields. Alternatively, you can return to the display of table MARA and check there whether the append is listed at the very end of the table.

Keep in mind that the name of the append ZSPORTS_APP as such is not relevant for the runtime. It will not be specified in the client application and it will not be visible when we check the field content of table MARA. Figure 2.17 shows table MARA in the background, with the list of appends in the dialog box. In the background, the name of our customer append is not visible in the list of fields.

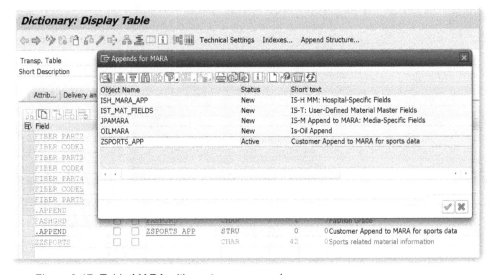

Figure 2.17: Table MARA with customer appends

Return to the entry screen of the ABAP Dictionary and display structure *BAPI_TE_MARA*. This structure contains the predefined field MATNR (CHAR 18) as the key field for the object StandardMaterial. Create an append as before, naming it *ZSPORTS_TE_MARA_APP*, again with the field ZZSPORTS (CHAR 42). Save and activate the append. The name of this append ZSPORTS_TE_MARA_APP is not relevant for the runtime either. Figure 2.18 shows the field ZZSPORTS as an append to table BAPI_TE_MARA.

Structure	BAPI_TE_MARA			Active			
Short Description	Customer-Defined Fields: Material Data at Client Level						

Attributes Components Entry help/check Currency/quantity fields

Predefined Type   1 / 3

Component	Typing Method	Component Type	Data Type	Length	Deci...	Short Description
MATERIAL	Types	▼ MATNR	CHAR	18	0	Material Number
.APPEND	Types	▼ ZSPORTS_TE_MARA_APP	(□□)	0	0	Customer Append to BAPI_TE_MARA for sports data
ZZSPORTS	Types	▼	CHAR	42	0	Sports related material information

Figure 2.18: Append for BAPI table extension structure

As an additional step, because the BAPI can be used to change existing objects, you have to create an identical append for the x structure BA-PI_TE_MARAX, but with type BAPIUPDATE for the field ZZSPORTS. During runtime, the field content must be set to *X*, as discussed before for x structures.

How can you check whether the content of your field is filled after the BAPI was called? One possibility is to use the Data Browser, so start transaction SE16. Enter *MARA* as the table name and press ⌈Enter⌋. A dialog box appears, as this table has too many fields for selection. Select the first five until *AENAM* and scroll at the end of the list to select your custom field *ZZSPORTS* (see Figure 2.19).

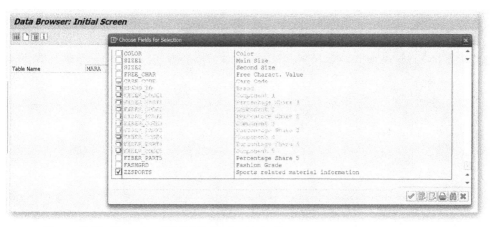

Figure 2.19: Choosing MARA fields for Data Browser

Confirm the dialog box with ⌈Enter⌋. On the selection screen, you should see your custom field listed as a parameter. If your system already contains entries in table MARA, none of these have content in your field as it is brand new. Note that although transaction MM03 can be used to display a material, this is not appropriate for us, as it does not consider the values of any table append.

Customizing activity required

 The use of customer fields for the BAPI SaveData requires an additional customizing activity in the Implementation Guide (IMG). You can find the respective entry by selecting LOGISTICS - GENERAL • MATERIAL MASTER • FIELD SELECTION • ASSIGN FIELDS TO FIELD SELECTION GROUP. Alternatively, you can use transaction OMSR for direct access to the customizing settings. You have to assign the customer fields to a field selection group to enable the transfer to the database as part of the BAPI processing.

Start transaction OMSR and select NEW ENTRIES. As the field name, enter the combination of *MARA* and your custom field, so in our case *MARA-ZZSPORTS*. In the MAINT. STATUS field in the FIELD ATTRIBUTES section, you should allow all possible values, so enter *ABCDEFGKLPQSVXZ* (use the F1 help to get the explanation of these values), as shown in Figure 2.20.

New Entries: Details of Added Entries

Field name   MARA-ZZSPORTS

Field attributes (industry and retail)
☐ Propose field cont.
Maint. status   ABCDEFGKLPQSVXZ
ALE field group

Field attributes (retail only)
Restrict matl cat.   No default
☐ Copy field content
☐ Incl. initial values

Figure 2.20: Details of the new material field MARA-ZZSPORTS

Keep the other fields at their default values. Save the settings, assigning a customizing request, and return to the CHANGE VIEW "FIELD GROUPS" OVERVIEW dialog box. Here, in the SELECTION GROUP field, you have to assign *111* as the selection group to your custom field *MARA-ZZSPORTS*, as shown in Figure 2.21.

Change View "Field Groups": Overview

New Entries

Field name in full	Short Description	Sel. group	
MARA-VOLTO	Excess Volume Tolerance of the Ha.	61	
MARA-VOLUM	Volume	86	
MARA-VPREH	Comparison price unit	153	
MARA-WEORA	Acceptance At Origin	124	
MARA-WESCH	Quantity: Number of GR/GI slips to .	88	
MARA-WHMATGR	Warehouse Material Group		
MARA-WHSTC	Warehouse Storage Condition		
MARA-WRKST	Basic Material	14	
MARA-XCHPF	Batch management requirement ind.	75	
MARA-XGCHP	Indicator: Approved batch record re.	75	
MARA-ZEIAR	Document type (without Document .	12	
MARA-ZEIFO	Page format of document (without .	12	
MARA-ZEINR	Document number (without docume.	108	
MARA-ZEIVR	Document version (without Docume.	12	
MARA-ZZSPORTS	Sports related material information	111	
MARA_LGHTY		45	

Figure 2.21: Assigning the selection group to the custom field

This finishes the preparation or design phase of our scenario. Now we must properly fill the input parameter EXTENSION_IN. It may also be a challenge to fill all required fields for the logistics BAPI—the parameters used in the following section may not fit the logistics customizing in your system in all cases. You can use transaction MM01 to create a material manually and note the required parameters.

Let's focus on the extension fields first, see Listing 2.4:

```
Data:
lt_extensionin TYPE STANDARD TABLE OF  bapiparex,
ls_extensionin type bapiparex,
lt_extensioninx TYPE STANDARD TABLE OF bapiparexx,
ls_extensioninx type bapiparexx.
```

```
...
MOVE 'BAPI_TE_MARA' TO ls_extensionin-structure.
ls_mara-material = ls_headdata-material.
ls_mara-ZZSPORTS = pa_value.
MOVE ls_mara TO ls_extensionin-valuepart1.
APPEND ls_extensionin to lt_extensionin.

MOVE 'BAPI_TE_MARAX' TO ls_extensioninx-structure.
ls_marax-material = ls_headdata-material.
ls_marax-ZZSPORTS = 'X'.
MOVE ls_marax TO ls_extensioninx-valuepart1.
APPEND ls_extensioninx to lt_extensioninx.
```

Listing 2.4: Filling the extension parts of the BAPI interface

The MOVE statement only fits if the length of all fields does not exceed the length 240 of the target field VALUEPART1.

A possible client application may look like Listing 2.5. (Note that you may have to adapt the material values to the settings for your system.)

```
REPORT  z_material_create.

DATA: ls_headdata      TYPE bapimathead,
      ls_clientdata    TYPE bapi_mara,
      ls_clientdatax   TYPE bapi_marax,
      lt_materialdescriptions TYPE TABLE OF bapi_makt,
      ls_mat_desc TYPE bapi_makt,
      ls_ret TYPE bapiret2,
      lt_mara TYPE STANDARD TABLE OF bapi_te_mara,
      ls_mara TYPE bapi_te_mara,
      lt_marax TYPE STANDARD TABLE OF bapi_te_marax,
      ls_marax TYPE bapi_te_marax,
      lv_mess(200).

DATA:
lt_extensionin TYPE STANDARD TABLE OF  bapiparex,
ls_extensionin TYPE bapiparex,
lt_extensioninx TYPE STANDARD TABLE OF bapiparexx,
ls_extensioninx TYPE bapiparexx.
```

```
PARAMETERS: pa_matnr(18), "not lower case!
pa_value(42) DEFAULT 'custom field' LOWER CASE,
pa_dest TYPE rfcdes-rfcdest DEFAULT 'FIRSTDEST'.

ls_headdata-material      = pa_matnr.
ls_headdata-ind_sector    = 'M'. " Mech. Engineering
ls_headdata-matl_type     = 'FERT'. " Finished product
ls_headdata-basic_view    = 'X'.
ls_clientdata-base_uom    = 'EA'. "Base unit of measure
ls_clientdatax-base_uom   = 'X'.

ls_mat_desc-langu = 'E'.
ls_mat_desc-matl_desc = 'Material description'.
APPEND ls_mat_desc TO lt_materialdescriptions.

**extension structure
MOVE 'BAPI_TE_MARA' TO ls_extensionin-structure.
ls_mara-material = ls_headdata-material.
ls_mara-zzsports = pa_value.
MOVE ls_mara TO ls_extensionin-valuepart1.
APPEND ls_extensionin TO lt_extensionin.

MOVE 'BAPI_TE_MARAX' TO ls_extensioninx-structure.
ls_marax-material = ls_headdata-material.
ls_marax-zzsports = 'X'.
MOVE ls_marax TO ls_extensioninx-valuepart1.
APPEND ls_extensioninx TO lt_extensioninx.

CALL FUNCTION 'BAPI_MATERIAL_SAVEDATA'
  DESTINATION pa_dest
  EXPORTING
    headdata              = ls_headdata
    clientdata            = ls_clientdata
    clientdatax           = ls_clientdatax
  IMPORTING
    return                = ls_ret
  TABLES
    materialdescription   = lt_materialdescriptions
    extensionin           = lt_extensionin
```

```
    extensioninx         = lt_extensioninx
  EXCEPTIONS
    system_failure       = 1 message lv_mess
    communication_failure = 2 MESSAGE lv_mess

      .


if sy-subrc ne 0.
  write: 'Call failed: ', lv_mess.
  exit.
  endif.
WRITE: 'Call executed'.

WRITE: ls_ret-id, ls_ret-message.
```

Listing 2.5: RFC client for extended BAPI call

Keep in mind that this is a simplified application in which we assume that all the DDIC objects of the target BAPI are present in the client system as well. This is probably not true for the structure and table appends.

You can check whether the fields of your custom append are filled using the Data Browser (transaction SE16). To display your new table MARA entry, click NEXT SCREEN as the field of the append is listed almost at the end of the field list.

What more can we have? Well, the other direction: let us see how the customer fields stored in the table append of table MARA can be seen when using a BAPI to read data.

Check the BAPI Explorer again for business object StandardMaterial to find the instance-dependent BAPI MaterialGetAll. Execute it in the target system, for example with a single test, and simply provide the material number. The result screen will show the table EXTENSIONOUT with one entry, which is the content of your custom field.

2.6 Creating customer BAPIs

You can create your own customer BAPI, which must include the creation of both the RFM as well as the business object type. Before we do so, it is worth thinking about the effort and the outcome.

The effort is higher than creating just the RFM, as you have to follow the BAPI development guidelines. On the other hand, these development guidelines are good practice for interface development in general. Therefore, even if you are not considering creating a customer BAPI, you should consider reading the following section to get an insight into some interface aspects we have not focused on yet.

Finally, a BAPI has broader visibility. This may be relevant especially for third-party software that is to be used in several systems.

The BAPI Explorer offers a separate PROJECT tab with helpful information for your project to allow you to create your own BAPI. We will use these principles but will follow a more pragmatic approach. The sequence is as follows:

1. **Model the business object type and BAPIs**
   Determine names for the object, methods, and key fields

2. **Create BAPI structures**
   Exclusive BAPI structures keep the BAPI interface stable

3. **Create the BAPI function module**
   Create the RFM following the BAPI naming and coding guidelines

4. **Create the BO, define the BAPI methods**
   Create the object and attach the BAPI methods

5. **Consider BAPI/ALE integration**
   Consider creating ALE objects for the BAPI

1. Model the business object type and BAPIs:

In this step, you model the names for the business object type and the BAPIs. In addition, the key fields for the object must be identified.

Our customer business object type will be named ZATHLETE, with a preceding Z to follow the namespace recommendation for customer objects. This object will have one key field, ATHLETE_ID, and three BAPI methods: GetList, GetDetail, CreateFromData. Only the method GetDetail will be instance-dependent, because only this method requires the key field to be provided as an import parameter. Note that the method CreateFromData does not require the key field as an import parameter, as we use the internal number range for a new ATHLETE_ID.

2. Create BAPI structures:

Separate BAPI structures must exist to keep the BAPI interface stable, as it is then independent of potential changes to any related structure.

Report BAPIFELD proposes BAPI field names

 You can use the report BAPIFELD to get a proposal for the BAPI field names. On the selection screen, specify the table definition *ZATHLETE* and execute the report. The PROPOSAL column shows the proposed names. We will nevertheless use slightly adapted names for our BAPI structure.

Use transaction SE11 to create a new structure ZBAPIATHLETE with the similar fields to table ZATHLETE but aligned to the naming proposals. The BAPI structure requires an additional field for the ISO representation of the country value, see Figure 2.22:

Structure	ZBAPIATHLETE	Active
Short Description	BAPI structure for athlete data	

Attributes / **Components** / Entry help/check / Currency/quantity fields

1 / 6

Component	Typing Method	Component Type	Data Type	Length	Deci...	Short Description
MANDT	Types	▼ MANDT	CLNT	3	0	Client
ATHLETE_ID	Types	▼ ZATHLETE_ID	NUMC	12	0	Identifier for athlete
NAME	Types	▼ ZNAME	CHAR	30	0	Name of athlete
DATE_OF_BIRTH	Types	▼ ZBIRTHDATE	DATS	8	0	Birthday of athlete
COUNTRY	Types	▼ LAND1	CHAR	3	0	Country Key
COUNTRYISO	Types	▼ INTCA	CHAR	2	0	Country ISO code

Figure 2.22: Structure ZBAPIATHLETE

Activate the new structure ZBAPIATHLETE.

Internal country representation is the leading factor

 The SAP internal representation for the country is decisive, as the database table ZATHLETE provides only this field. This means that if only the ISO field is provided from the client for the creation of a new object, the BAPI implementation will calculate the internal representation using the function module COUNTRY_CODE_ISO_TO_SAP.

For reading data, the ISO value will be calculated from the internal value using the function module COUNTRY_CODE_SAP_TO_ISO.

3. Create BAPI function modules:

Although you can start from scratch, you may as well simply copy our existing RFMs to the respective BAPI modules (and adapt the copies). Use the naming convention for BAPIs and save the new modules in the existing package ZSPORTS:

```
Z_ATHLETES_LIST -> ZBAPI_ATHLETE_GETLIST

Z_ATHLETE_READ_DETAILS -> ZBAPI_ATHLETE_GETDETAIL

Z_CREATE_ATHLETE -> ZBAPI_ATHLETE_CREATEFROMDATA
```

There are some generic adaptations that are relevant for all three BAPIs, as listed below:

- ▶ Interface: use the BAPI structure ZBAPIATHLETE instead of the references to the table definition or to data structures.
- ▶ Interface: add an EXPORTING parameter RETURN referencing BAPIRET2.
- ▶ Interface: remove the exceptions.
- ▶ Coding: fill RETURN with the respective information by using function module BALW_BAPIRETURN_GET2.
- ▶ Coding: provide content for ISO fields.
- ▶ Documentation: create documentation for all parameters and for the BAPI modules.

▶ Status: switch to the ATTRIBUTES tab and release the modules by selecting FUNCTION MODULE • RELEASE • RELEASE.

▶ Status: activate the modules.

An additional aspect is only relevant if you are working on a copy of our existing RFMs. You can delete the prefix *RFM* in the field SHORT TEXT (tab ATTRIBUTES), as all BAPI modules are RFMs implicitly anyway.

Each of our three BAPIs requires specific adaptations which are discussed in the following paragraphs.

We start with ZBAPI_ATHLETE_GETDETAIL. First, we switch the references for the interface parameters to the structure ZBAPIATHLETE. Then, in the coding, we have to consider providing the ISO representation of the country, as this value is not stored in the database table. This is achieved by a local call to the function module COUNTRY_CODE_SAP_TO_ISO. Finally, the replacement of exceptions with the export parameter RETURN is achieved via a local call to BALW_BAPIRETURN_GET2, which fills the structure RETURN. It is not required, but it is good style to fill RETURN-TYPE with *S* as a success message at the end. As we are filling only one field, the function module BALW_BAPIRETURN_GET2 is not required.

Listing 2.6 shows the adapted source code.

```
FUNCTION ZBAPI_ATHLETE_GETDETAIL .
*"----------------------------------------------------------
*"*"Local Interface:
*"  IMPORTING
*"     VALUE(I_ATHLETE_ID) TYPE  ZBAPIATHLETE-ATHLETE_ID
*"  EXPORTING
*"     VALUE(E_NAME) TYPE  ZBAPIATHLETE-NAME
*"     VALUE(E_DATE_OF_BIRTH) TYPE  ZBAPIATHLETE-DATE_OF_BIRTH
*"     VALUE(E_COUNTRY) TYPE  ZBAPIATHLETE-COUNTRY
*"     VALUE(E_COUNTRY_ISO) TYPE  ZBAPIATHLETE-COUNTRYISO
*"     VALUE(RETURN) TYPE  BAPIRET2
*"----------------------------------------------------------

    DATA: ls_athlete TYPE zbapiathlete.
```

```
* Authority check
  AUTHORITY-CHECK OBJECT 'ZATHLETE'
            ID 'ACTVT' FIELD '03'.
  IF sy-subrc NE 0.
    CALL FUNCTION 'BALW_BAPIRETURN_GET2'
      EXPORTING
        type   = 'E'
        cl     = 'ZSPORTS'
        number = '001'
        PAR1   = 'missing_authorization'
      IMPORTING
        return = return.
    EXIT.
  ENDIF.

* Consistency checks
  IF i_athlete_id IS INITIAL.
    CALL FUNCTION 'BALW_BAPIRETURN_GET2'
      EXPORTING
        type   = 'E'
        cl     = 'ZSPORTS'
        number = '001'
        PAR1   = 'invalid_data'
      IMPORTING
        return = return.
    EXIT.
  ENDIF.

  SELECT SINGLE * FROM zathlete INTO ls_athlete WHERE
    athlete_id = i_athlete_id.

  IF sy-subrc NE 0.
    CALL FUNCTION 'BALW_BAPIRETURN_GET2'
      EXPORTING
        type   = 'E'
        cl     = 'ZSPORTS'
        number = '001'
        PAR1   = 'invalid_id'
      IMPORTING
        return = return.
```

165

```
    EXIT.
  ENDIF.

CALL FUNCTION 'COUNTRY_CODE_SAP_TO_ISO'
  EXPORTING
    sap_code       = ls_athlete-country
  IMPORTING
    ISO_CODE       = ls_athlete-countryiso
  EXCEPTIONS
    NOT_FOUND      = 1
    OTHERS         = 2
             .
  IF sy-subrc NE 0.
    CALL FUNCTION 'BALW_BAPIRETURN_GET2'
      EXPORTING
        type   = 'E'
        cl     = 'ZSPORTS'
        number = '001'
        PAR1   = 'conversion error'
      IMPORTING
        return = return.
    EXIT.
  ENDIF.

  e_name = ls_athlete-name.
  e_date_of_birth = ls_athlete-date_of_birth.
  e_country = ls_athlete-country.
  e_country_iso = ls_athlete-countryiso.

  return-type = 'S'.

ENDFUNCTION.
```

Listing 2.6: Source code for ZBAPI_ATHLETE_GETDETAIL

Release the BAPI and activate it. If it is not released, it cannot be used later for the business object.

Next is ZBAPI_ATHLETE_GETLIST: in addition to the adaptation in the TABLES section (referencing ZBAPIATHLETE instead of ZATHLETE), the importing parameter I_MAX_READ must reference a BAPI field. We use BAPISFLAUX-BAPIMAXROW for this.

Compared to the previous BAPI GetDetail, we now have multiple country fields to convert, so we use a LOOP statement. In the loop, we also move the fields for the respective table line (sometimes called work area) from the database representation to the external BAPI representation which includes the ISO field.

Check these aspects in Listing 2.7.

```
FUNCTION zbapi_athlete_getlist .
*"----------------------------------------------------------------
*"*"Local Interface:
*"  IMPORTING
*"     VALUE(I_MAX_READ) TYPE  BAPISFLAUX-
*"     BAPIMAXROW DEFAULT 0
*"  EXPORTING
*"     VALUE(RETURN) TYPE  BAPIRET2
*"  TABLES
*"     ATHLETES_LIST STRUCTURE  ZBAPIATHLETE
*"----------------------------------------------------------------

  DATA: ls_athlete TYPE zathlete,
        lt_athletes TYPE TABLE OF zathlete,
        ls_bapiathlete TYPE zbapiathlete.

* Authority check
  AUTHORITY-CHECK OBJECT 'ZATHLETE'
               ID 'ACTVT' FIELD '03'.
  IF sy-subrc NE 0.
    CALL FUNCTION 'BALW_BAPIRETURN_GET2'
      EXPORTING
        type   = 'E'
        cl     = 'ZSPORTS'
        number = '001'
        par1   = 'missing_authorization'
      IMPORTING
        return = return.
    EXIT.
  ENDIF.
```

```
  CLEAR athletes_list.
* DB access
  SELECT * FROM zathlete INTO TABLE lt_athletes
    UP TO i_max_read ROWS   .
  IF sy-subrc NE 0.
    CALL FUNCTION 'BALW_BAPIRETURN_GET2'
      EXPORTING
        type   = 'E'
        cl     = 'ZSPORTS'
        number = '001'
        par1   = 'error during database access'
      IMPORTING
        return = return.
    EXIT.
  ENDIF.

* Transfer to external structure, consider ISO field
  LOOP AT lt_athletes INTO ls_athlete.
    MOVE-CORRESPONDING ls_athlete TO ls_bapiathlete.
    IF NOT ls_athlete-country IS INITIAL.
      CALL FUNCTION 'COUNTRY_CODE_SAP_TO_ISO'
        EXPORTING
          sap_code = ls_athlete-country
        IMPORTING
          iso_code = ls_bapiathlete-countryiso
        EXCEPTIONS
          not_found = 1
          OTHERS    = 2.
      IF sy-subrc <> 0.
        CALL FUNCTION 'BALW_BAPIRETURN_GET2'
          EXPORTING
            type   = 'E'
            cl     = 'ZSPORTS'
            number = '001'
            par1   = 'error during ISO provisioning'
          IMPORTING
            return = return.
        EXIT.
      ENDIF.
    ENDIF.
```

```
     APPEND ls_bapiathlete TO athletes_list.
     CLEAR ls_bapiathlete.
   ENDLOOP.
   return-type = 'S'.
 ENDFUNCTION.
```

Listing 2.7: Source code for ZBAPI_ATHLETE_GETLIST

For ZBAPI_ATHLETE_CREATEFROMDATA, remove the input parameter I_DO_COMMIT, as BAPIs do not execute the commit anyway. With regard to the values for the country, we have to check whether the internal value is provided. If not, the ISO value is used and converted to the internal country representation. If both are missing, the BAPI will return a corresponding error message.

We put the RETURN parameter into the TABLES section to allow several messages. This allows us to check all input parameters and provide the results in the first call. This ensures that the client does not get just one error message, fixes the value, and then gets the next error only after the second call.

TEST_RUN parameter for BAPIs that create objects

 Some BAPIs for creating new objects offer an additional import parameter TEST_RUN with associated type BAPIS-FLAUX-TESTRUN. It can be used to only check the input values; without it, executing the BAPI will store the data on the database.

You might think that to do this, you can omit the subsequent COMMIT WORK statement, which is added externally. Correct, but this would create an entry in the update table. And this entry remains if you do not finish your test with an external execution of BAPI_TRANSACTION _ROLLBACK—which means that it is easier to use the TEST_RUN parameter, agreed?

See the following proposal for our third BAPI implementation, Listing 2.8.

```
FUNCTION zbapi_athlete_createfromdata .
*"----------------------------------------------------------------
*"*"Local Interface:
```

```
*"  IMPORTING
*"     VALUE(I_ATHLETE_NAME) TYPE  ZBAPIATHLETE-NAME
*"     VALUE(I_DATE_OF_BIRTH) TYPE  ZBAPIATHLETE-DATE_OF_BIRTH
*"     VALUE(I_COUNTRY) TYPE  ZBAPIATHLETE-COUNTRY
*"     VALUE(I_COUNTRY_ISO) TYPE  ZBAPIATHLETE-COUNTRYISO
*"     VALUE(I_TEST_RUN) TYPE  BAPISFLAUX-TESTRUN
*"  TABLES
*"     RETURN STRUCTURE  BAPIRET2 OPTIONAL
*"----------------------------------------------------------
  DATA: lv_athlete_id TYPE zbapiathlete-athlete_id,
        lv_athlete_id_char(50),
        lv_land TYPE land1,
        lv_errflag TYPE boolean.


  lv_errflag = abap_false.

* Authority check
  AUTHORITY-CHECK OBJECT 'ZATHLETE'
           ID 'ACTVT' FIELD '01'.
  IF sy-subrc NE 0.
    CALL FUNCTION 'BALW_BAPIRETURN_GET2'
      EXPORTING
        type  = 'E'
        cl    = 'ZSPORTS'
        number = '002'
        par1  = 'missing_authorization'
      IMPORTING
        return = return.
    APPEND return.
    EXIT.
  ENDIF.


*Consistency checks, separated
  IF i_athlete_name IS INITIAL .
    CALL FUNCTION 'BALW_BAPIRETURN_GET2'
      EXPORTING
        type  = 'E'
        cl    = 'ZSPORTS'
        number = '003'
        par1  = 'name not specified'
      IMPORTING
```

```
        return = return.
    APPEND return.
    lv_errflag = abap_true.
ENDIF.

IF i_date_of_birth IS INITIAL .
    CALL FUNCTION 'BALW_BAPIRETURN_GET2'
        EXPORTING
            type   = 'E'
            cl     = 'ZSPORTS'
            number = '003'
            par1   = 'date not specified'
        IMPORTING
            return = return.
    APPEND return.
    lv_errflag = abap_true.
ENDIF.


CALL FUNCTION 'DATE_CHECK_PLAUSIBILITY'
    EXPORTING
        date                       = i_date_of_birth
    EXCEPTIONS
        plausibility_check_failed = 1
        OTHERS                     = 2.
IF sy-subrc NE 0.
    CALL FUNCTION 'BALW_BAPIRETURN_GET2'
        EXPORTING
            type   = 'E'
            cl     = 'ZSPORTS'
            number = '003'
            par1   = 'date format wrong'
        IMPORTING
            return = return.
    APPEND return.
    lv_errflag = abap_true.
ENDIF.

IF i_country IS INITIAL AND i_country_iso IS INITIAL.
    CALL FUNCTION 'BALW_BAPIRETURN_GET2'
        EXPORTING
            type   = 'E'
```

```
        cl      = 'ZSPORTS'
        number = '003'
        parl    = 'country not specified'
      IMPORTING
        return = return.
    APPEND return.
    lv_errflag = abap_true.
  ENDIF.

* country handling:
  IF i_country IS NOT INITIAL.
    SELECT SINGLE land1 FROM t005 INTO lv_land
                        WHERE land1 = i_country.

    IF sy-subrc NE 0.
      CALL FUNCTION 'BALW_BAPIRETURN_GET2'
        EXPORTING
          type    = 'E'
          cl      = 'ZSPORTS'
          number = '003'
          parl    = 'country not valid'
        IMPORTING
          return = return.
      APPEND return.
      lv_errflag = abap_true.
    ENDIF.
  ELSE.
* Here, country_iso is not initial
    CALL FUNCTION 'COUNTRY_CODE_ISO_TO_SAP'
      EXPORTING
        iso_code  = i_country_iso
      IMPORTING
        sap_code  = i_country
*       UNIQUE    =
      EXCEPTIONS
        not_found = 1
        OTHERS    = 2.
    IF sy-subrc <> 0.
      CALL FUNCTION 'BALW_BAPIRETURN_GET2'
        EXPORTING
          type    = 'E'
```

```
            cl     = 'ZSPORTS'
            number = '001'
            par1   = 'country conversion error'
         IMPORTING
            return = return.
       APPEND return.
       lv_errflag = abap_true.
    ENDIF.
  ENDIF.

  IF lv_errflag = abap_true.
    EXIT.
  ENDIF.

  IF i_test_run IS INITIAL.

* Locking
    CALL FUNCTION 'ENQUEUE_EZATHLETE'
      EXPORTING
*       MODE_ZATHLETE  = 'E'
        mandt          = sy-mandt
*       athlete_id     = i_athlete_id
*       X_ATHLETE_ID   = ' '
*       _SCOPE         = '2'
*       _WAIT          = ' '
*       _COLLECT       = ' '
      EXCEPTIONS
        foreign_lock   = 1
        system_failure = 2
        OTHERS         = 3.
    IF sy-subrc <> 0.
      CALL FUNCTION 'BALW_BAPIRETURN_GET2'
        EXPORTING
          type   = 'E'
          cl     = 'ZSPORTS'
          number = '005'
          par1   = 'object locked'
        IMPORTING
          return = return.
      APPEND return.
      EXIT.
```

```
          ENDIF.

      CALL FUNCTION 'NUMBER_GET_NEXT'
        EXPORTING
          nr_range_nr              = '1'
          object                   = 'ZATHLETE'
        IMPORTING
          number                   = lv_athlete_id
        EXCEPTIONS
          interval_not_found       = 1
          number_range_not_intern  = 2
          object_not_found         = 3
          quantity_is_0            = 4
          quantity_is_not_1        = 5
          interval_overflow        = 6
          buffer_overflow          = 7
          OTHERS                   = 8.
      IF sy-subrc <> 0.
        CALL FUNCTION 'BALW_BAPIRETURN_GET2'
          EXPORTING
            type   = 'E'
            cl     = 'ZSPORTS'
            number = '001'
            par1   = 'error while getting next ID'
          IMPORTING
            return = return.
        APPEND return.
        EXIT.
      ENDIF.

      CALL FUNCTION 'Z_SAVE_ATHLETE'
        IN UPDATE TASK
        EXPORTING
          i_athlete_name  = i_athlete_name
          i_date_of_birth = i_date_of_birth
          i_country       = i_country
          i_athlete_id    = lv_athlete_id.
      IF sy-subrc NE 0. " error in update task
        CALL FUNCTION 'BALW_BAPIRETURN_GET2'
          EXPORTING
            type   = 'E'
```

```
            cl     = 'ZSPORTS'
            number = '001'
            parl   = 'error during update task creation'
        IMPORTING
            return = return.
      APPEND return.
      EXIT.
    ELSE.
      WRITE lv_athlete_id to lv_athlete_id_char.
      CALL FUNCTION 'BALW_BAPIRETURN_GET2'
        EXPORTING
            type   = 'S'
            cl     = 'ZSPORTS'
            number = '000'
            parl   = 'New athlete was stored '
            par2   = lv_athlete_id_char
        IMPORTING
            return = return.
      APPEND return.
    ENDIF.
  ELSE. " test run
    CALL FUNCTION 'BALW_BAPIRETURN_GET2'
      EXPORTING
          type   = 'I'
          cl     = 'ZSPORTS'
          number = '000'
          parl   = 'BAPi was executed in test run'
      IMPORTING
          return = return.
    APPEND return.
  ENDIF.
ENDFUNCTION.
```

Listing 2.8: Customer BAPI for creating an athlete

Note that the existing update module Z_SAVE_ATHLETE is used as before but the subsequent COMMIT WORK statement is removed from the RFM.

Remember that all parameters and also the function modules must be documented. Check again that you have activated and released all three

BAPI modules. If they are not released, they cannot be used later for the business object.

4. Create the BO, define the BAPI methods:

Instead of using the *Business Object Builder* (transaction SWO1), we create the object directly from the ABAP workbench. Use the context menu (right mouse-click) on the package ZSPORTS and choose CREATE • BUSINESS ENGINEERING • BUSINESS OBJECT TYPE.

A dialog box CREATE OBJECT TYPE appears. Enter the parameters as shown in Figure 2.23. We will stick to the following naming conventions:

▶ Object type name stays in the customer namespace

▶ Object name starts with Z_

▶ Program name starts with ZR

Figure 2.23: Creating a business object type

Press ⌈Enter⌉ and assign the object to a transport package (not $TMP) otherwise it cannot be released later.

Now the new object type *ZATHLETE* is shown in the Business Object Builder. For our BAPI scenario, not all aspects are relevant, only the key fields and the methods. You can expand the folder METHODS to see that two methods are assigned per default. They are highlighted in red because they have not been implemented yet (see Figure 2.24)—and they do not have to be implemented.

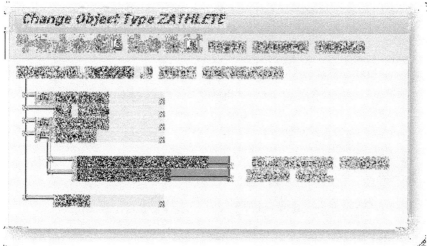

Figure 2.24: Initial business object type ZATHLETE

Add documentation for the object: Choose GOTO • DOCUMENTATION (or click the 🔲 icon) and enter the documentation for the object. Save it and return to the object display.

Add the key field ID: Select the line KEY FIELDS and press F5 to create a key field. In the dialog box CREATE KEY FIELD, select *No* to not use a DDIC proposal. In the KEY FIELD dialog box, enter *Athlete_ID* in the KEY FIELD, NAME and DESCRIPTION fields. Specify the structure *ZBAPIATH-LETE* in the REFERENCE TABLE field and use the input help F4 to select *ATHLETE_ID* for the field REFERENCE FIELD, as shown in Figure 2.25.

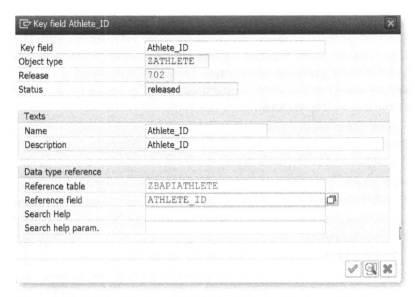

Figure 2.25: Defining the key field Athlete_ID for the business object

Press Enter to close the dialog box. Save the business object.

Add the RFMs as BAPI methods: Choose UTILITIES • API METHODS • ADD METHOD. In the dialog box that appears, specify *ZBAPI_ ATHLETE_GETLIST* as the first method and press Enter. The dialog box is expanded with a proposal for the method name and the texts. Adapt the text in the NAME field, as it may be cut off (see Figure 2.26).

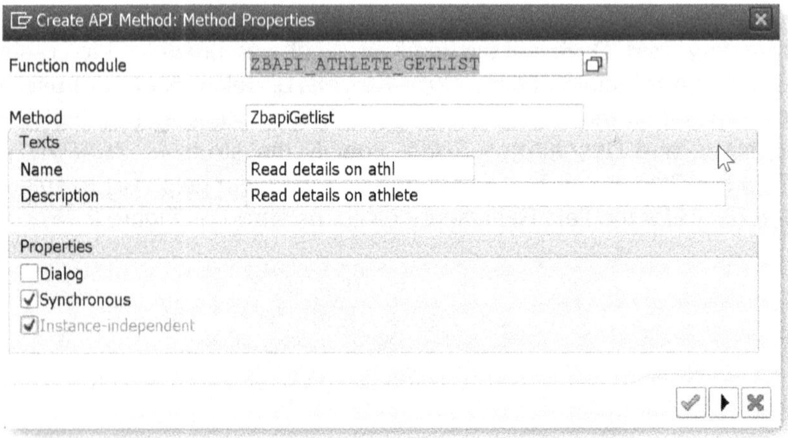

Figure 2.26: Method properties for creating an API method

Click the icon ▶ NEXT STEP to proceed to the step CREATE PARAMETERS. In this step, you can be more specific with the parameters compared to the RFM. In our case, the table ATHLETES_LIST is defined in the TABLES section, but only **exports** data. Therefore, de-select the IMPORT checkbox for this line, as shown in Figure 2.27.

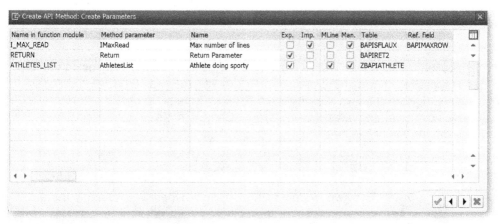

Figure 2.27: Parameter definition for BAPI assignment to object

Again, click ▶ to display a dialog box EXTEND PROGRAM (see Figure 2.28).

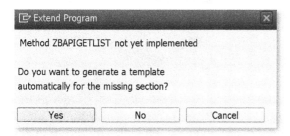

Figure 2.28: Extending the business object with a template

Confirm the dialog box with *Yes* so that a template is created for the missing section.

Repeat this procedure to assign the other RFMs. First assign ZBA-PI_ATHLETE_GETDETAIL as the method ZbapiGetDetail. Note that during the initial assignment, you cannot deselect the attribute INSTANCE-INDEPENDENT (compare Figure 2.26). After the assignment, you can double-click the method name and manually deselect the attribute INSTANCE-

INDEPENDENT. This is relevant for the display of the method afterwards in transaction BAPI.

Then assign ZBAPI_ATHLETE_CREATEFROMDATA as the method ZbapiCreateFromData. Ignore the warning in the BAPI CONSISTENCY CHECKS dialog box about missing input help. In the CREATE PARAMETERS dialog box, deselect the IMPORT checkbox for the parameter RETURN, as it is only exported by the RFM.

Set the object status first to *Implemented*, then to *Released* by using the respective entries in the menu EDIT • CHANGE RELEASE STATUS • OBJECT TYPE. Ignore the two warnings NO DEFAULT ATTRIBUTE DEFINED FOR THE OBJECT TYPE and METHOD 'EXISTENCECHECK' IS NOT REDEFINED. Then generate the object by choosing OBJECT TYPE • GENERATE.

Avoiding the warnings

The two warnings that appear when you change the release status of the object are not relevant for us. Nevertheless, you may still want to avoid them.

Select the method EXISTENCECHECK and then EDIT • REDEFINE. Then choose OBJECTTYPE • CHECK and confirm the EXTEND PROGRAM dialog box to generate a template. Save the template without changing the code and then exit the editor.

Via the menu GOTO • BASIC DATA, choose the DEFAULTS tab and use the F4 help to set the default attribute to *Athlete_ID*.

Set the status of all three methods to *Released* via EDIT • CHANGE RELEASE STATUS • OBJECT TYPE COMPONENT • TO RELEASED. Note the small checkmark at the end of the method name as the indicator for the method being released, as shown in Figure 2.29.

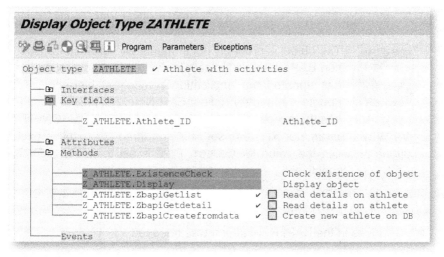

Figure 2.29: Final view of the definition of the business object with BAPIs

Save the object and switch to display mode. Finally, you can check whether your custom business object is listed in transaction BAPI.

Figure 2.30 shows how the object is displayed. Check whether your BAPI ZbapiGetDetail is shown as instance-dependent.

Figure 2.30: Displaying a customer business object in transaction BAPI

Object display in transaction BAPI

 The object is probably not immediately visible in transaction BAPI. It takes typically a day until a background job has updated the application component hierarchy. To update it manually, follow SAP Note 706195—it describes the execution of function module RS_COMPONENT _VIEW with parameter REFRESH set to *X* and three consecutive executions in which the value for OBJECT_TYPE is set to *APPL*, *DEVC*, and *SOBJ* respectively.

▶ Changes in the BAPI RFM after it was released

You may adapt the source code if the interface is not affected. If adaptations to the interface are required, they should only add optional parameters. Consider creating a second BAPI instead with the new interface and use the number suffix in the name of the BAPI.

If interface adaptations really are required, you must first set the RFM to status *Not Released*. You can then adapt the interface section of the RFM. Once the adaptation is finished, set the status of the RFM back to *Released*. You also have to set the status of the business object method back to *Implemented* and then to *Released* once again.

▶ Using the business object HelpValues

Now that we have our own BAPIs, we can examine the methods of the BAPI service object HelpValues which was already mentioned in Section 2.4.

The scenario is that your client application will provide support for the user. If the user wants to know which values are possible for a field, the SAPGUI offers the F4 help. In your client application, you may want to offer a similar help. Therefore, you have to ask the target system for the help values and to do this, you use the method HelpValues.GetList.

Let's use the method GetList on the parameter Country of the BAPI Zathlete.ZbapiGetDetails to get a list of help values for this field Country. In transaction BAPI, look for the business object *HelpValues*, open the method *GetList*, and from the TOOLS tab, select FUNCTION BUILDER and execute a single test. (Yes, that was a long description of executing a test for function module BAPI_HELPVALUES_GET in the Function Builder.)

It is important that you enable the UPPERCASE/LOWERCASE checkbox because the name of the method is case sensitive! In the OBJTYPE field, enter *ZATHLETE*, in the METHOD field specify *ZbapiGetList*, and in the PARAMETER field, enter *ECountry*. Execute the test and you will find the help values in the table HELPVALUES (use the 𝄞 icon to see the content, see Figure 2.31).

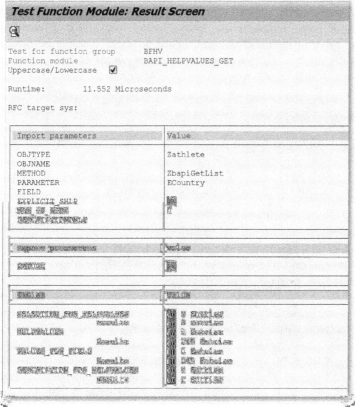

Figure 2.31: Using BAPI HelpValues for a BAPI parameter

Fields PARAMETER and FIELD

Note that the field FIELD is only relevant if a field inside a structure is to be referenced: in that case, PARAMETER is the name of the structure and FIELD is the name of the field in the structure.

The next step would be to create a client application that remotely executes one of our customer BAPIs, for example ZBAPI_ATHLETE_CREATEFROMDATA (followed by a remote call to BAPI_TRANSACTION_COMMIT). We will leave this exercise to you, as there is nothing different to consider compared to the discussions we have already had on BAPI clients. The biggest hurdle is probably working with the structures that are only defined in the target system.

It looks as if we have discussed all relevant aspects of the BAPI so that you can use this interface technology in your projects. But wait, there is one important aspect of BAPIs that you must be aware of: the potential conflict of error handling with asynchronous BAPI calls such as bgRFC!

Asynchronous calls and BAPI error handling

Here, two concepts collide: asynchronous technologies, such as bgRFC, with their advantage of exactly-once execution, and the BAPI error concept of using the parameter RETURN instead of exceptions.

We have discussed asynchronous techniques with their behavior to return only errors but no business data. But BAPIs do not offer exceptions! Therefore, if a bgRFC call reaches the server, and the BAPI returns an error in the parameter RETURN, no one cares! This information is not returned to the client.

So how do we handle this? We have two proposals.

One possible approach is as follows: you first execute a synchronous call to the BAPI to get all data checked for consistency but you do not trigger the `COMMIT WORK` statement. Instead, you send a call to BAPI_TRANSACTION_ROLLBACK. If all data is accepted, you follow up with the asynchronous call (using bgRFC). However, this will still not catch situations in which an error came up in-between, after the synchronous check and the asynchronous call. That can be an error independent of your data, such as the log table being full.

The other approach is to use ALE and IDocs, which even works for some BAPI calls. And this leads us nicely into the next chapter on ALE and IDocs, doesn't it?

3 IDocs and ALE

SAP provides an asynchronous interface technology with all required artefacts out of the box. For interface developers, it is essential to understand the concept of this technology and to appreciate
the potential of the concept.

3.1 Introducing IDocs

We follow up where we left you in a puzzled state, at the end of the last
chapter: what about ALE, IDocs, and their relationship to BAPIs? And
how do they solve the catch-22 situation of asynchronous calls and missing exceptions in BAPIs, mentioned at the very end of Section 2.6.

Looking at Figure 2.3 again, you will see a special BAPI attribute that we
have not discussed yet but now the time has come to introduce it: the *ALE
message type*. An ALE message type provides an interface for sending an
IDoc instead of a BAPI request—this is fine, but what is an IDoc?

An IDoc is a data package that is exchanged between systems (ABAP
and even non-ABAP systems). IDoc is the abbreviation for *intermediate
document*, and communication using an IDoc is always asynchronous.
But, we have been exchanging data between systems since we started
with the first chapter, so what is so special here?

The big advantage of this technology is that SAP provides all required
features and tools to enable data transfer out of the box, without the need
for any development: only configuration is required. (**No development?**
But keep reading, as we have some development aspects for you!)

ALE: Application Link Enabling

 ALE (Application Link Enabling) is the term that comprises all of the following in an ABAP system:

▶ interface definitions (including versioning),

▶ protocol support,

▶ client applications,

▶ server applications,

▶ monitoring infrastructure,

▶ testing capabilities,

▶ extension capability.

While a typical introduction to ALE and IDocs will explain all of this, focusing on how to enable system communication **without** ABAP development, we will use another approach and discuss the special case of using an ABAP report to send an IDoc. This approach will explain all the required steps and terms and will stick to a use case that may be relevant for you as an ABAP developer.

And even as an ABAP developer, it is important to be aware of the advantages of ALE. Some scenarios may be supported by SAP out of the box without any development effort, which can speed up the implementation of these scenarios.

What on Earth is an SAP IDoc?

 For further details, see the book *What on Earth is an SAP IDoc?* (Jelena Perfiljeva, Espresso Tutorials, 2016).

3.2   Relating BAPIs and IDocs

We start with the scenario we discussed at the end of the last chapter. When using an asynchronous technique (e.g., bgRFC) to send a BAPI, what happens if the BAPI returns an error message in the parameter RETURN? The BAPI does not throw an exception, so the ABAP runtime in the target system does not indicate an error, and the source system is not notified. Remember that asynchronous techniques only report those errors in the server system back to the client system that are based on explicit RFM exceptions.

The solution for this dilemma is to send an IDoc instead of the BAPI call. This is simple if the ALE interface has already been defined for the BAPI. It comprises a function module that you call locally in the source system, instead of a remote call to the BAPI. And for IDocs, it is possible to request a status update at a later point in time.

ALE message type only for BAPIs that change data

 As mentioned, IDocs are exchanged only asynchronously. Therefore, it only makes sense to think about using IDocs for those BAPIs that change something in the target database. Asynchronous communication does not provide a business response, so there is no sense in using a BAPI which requests data from the target system asynchronously.

3.3   Using ALE interfaces for BAPIs

The ALE message type may be part of the BAPI definition, at least for those BAPIs which change data in the target system. We will start with an existing example and will discuss the possibility for creating this type of ALE message type for custom BAPIs later.

We use our first business object type *USER* again (as in Figure 2.2) and display the details of the BAPI *Clone*, see Figure 3.1.

Figure 3.1: ALE message type example for BAPI_USER_CLONE

Let's check the details: double-click the name of the ALE message type. This will forward navigate you to transaction BDBG, with the respective data for our BAPI already entered.

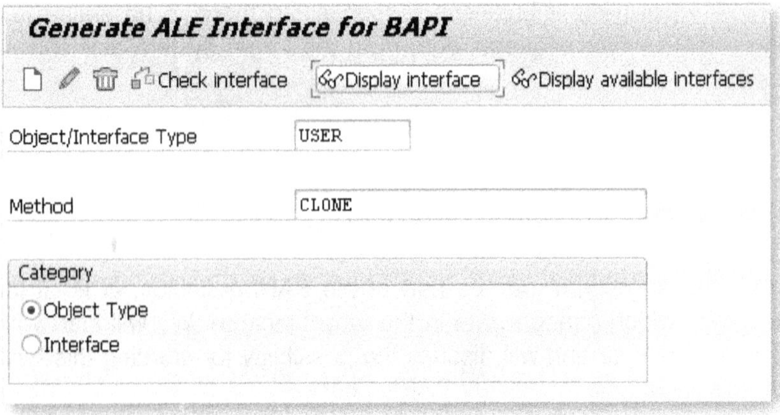

Generate ALE Interface for BAPI

☐ ✎ 🗑 ✇Check interface ✇Display interface ✇Display available interfaces

Object/Interface Type   USER

Method   CLONE

Category
◉ Object Type
○ Interface

Figure 3.2: Transaction BDBG: ALE interface for User.Clone

ALE interface or ALE message type

 In the BAPI Explorer, the details for a BAPI show the attribute ALE MESSAGE TYPE. The title of transaction BDBG refers to ALE INTERFACE. What is the difference?

The term *ALE interface* is a bundle for several objects. One of these is the *ALE message type*, which is a kind of business classification for the data transferred in the IDoc. Other objects of the ALE interface are introduced in the following paragraphs.

Now click DISPLAY INTERFACE (see Figure 3.2 above) to display the list of all objects of the ALE interface. Note that the design of the results list may look different in your system, as the kind of display depends on the release. However, the content is the same: the list shows all the objects that belong to the ALE interface. Note that you may have to scroll down to see the function modules shown in Figure 3.3.

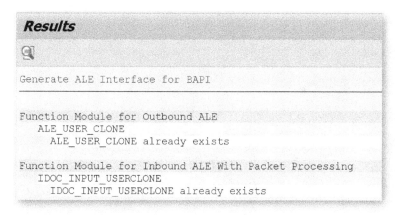

Figure 3.3: ALE interface parts for BAPI_USER_CLONE

The ALE interface consists of some structure objects that we will discuss later (not shown in Figure 3.3 above) and two function modules: one for outbound ALE and one for inbound ALE. The outbound ALE module can be used in the source system to create an IDoc; the inbound ALE module will be used in the target system to receive and process the IDoc.

ALE interfaces required in the source and target

When you send an RFC request to a target system to execute an RFM, the RFM as such does not have to exist in the source system. For ALE, this is different: as a minimum, the IDoc structure objects of the ALE message interface must exist in both the source and target systems.

The inbound ALE module does not have to exist in the source system—and vice versa: the outbound module is not required in the target system. However, as we are using transaction BDBG to create the objects, the modules will be there in the respective system as well.

Click the name of the outbound ALE module *ALE_USER_CLONE* to display the function module. Compare the interface with *BAPI_USER_CLONE* and you will see that they are almost identical. The ALE module simply offers additional parameters that are IDoc-related, as shown in Figure 3.4.

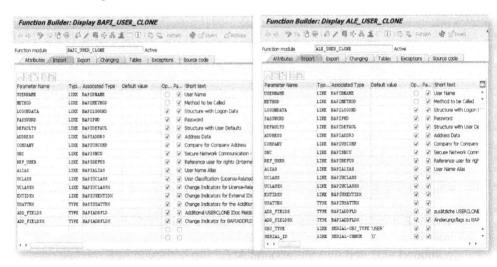

Figure 3.4: Comparing BAPI and ALE modules for User.Clone

We will discuss additional table parameters that are not visible in Figure 3.4 shortly.

So what does an IDoc look like? Let's create one quickly to examine it. To do this, we execute a test for the ALE outbound module.

Start the test environment of the Function Builder for the module ALE_USER_CLONE. Before executing the test, specify your user ID in the field USERNAME and add an entry with the value *RECEIVER* in table RECEIVERS. Then execute the test.

ALE outbound module requires a logical system

If the execution of the test for ALE_USER_CLONE fails with an error message LOGICAL SYSTEM NAME IS NOT DEFINED. some basic configuration is missing—the current client has no *logical system* name assigned. We will cover the configuration later.

If you do receive this error message, jump forward to Section 3.5 and do some configuration now. You have to maintain a logical system name (defined in transaction BD54) for your current client using transaction SCC4.

On the results screen, check which parameters have changed: table COMMUNICATION_DOCUMENTS now has one entry. If you display the details, you will see that one IDoc has been created and the object key is listed. So we have created an IDoc. But where can we check the details of the IDoc?

Transaction BD87 is the STATUS MONITOR FOR ALE MESSAGES—it is one of the monitoring transactions for checking IDocs. When you start the transaction, you will see your IDoc listed, as you can see in Figure 3.5.

Status Monitor for ALE Messages

🎛 🗐 🗒 ⬛ 🗂 🔽 Select IDocs   🔍Display IDocs   🖳Trace IDocs   ⏳Process

IDocs	IDoc Status	Number
・ 🔽 IDoc selection		
- 🖼 Athlete data		1
・ 🖺 IDocs in outbound processing		1
・ ◎ Error in ALE service	29	1
・ 🗂 USERCLONE		1

Figure 3.5: IDoc in error state in transaction BD87

193

The IDoc is listed with an error, as some ALE configuration is missing. So far, we have only specified the name of the receiver but no details such as an RFC destination. Note that for IDoc delivery, other communication protocols are possible in addition to RFC. Nevertheless, we have an IDoc that we can analyze.

Double-click the name *USERCLONE* to get to the IDOC SELECTION display, in which you again double-click the IDoc number. This will display the details of the IDoc. On the left hand side, we see the three parts of an IDoc: CONTROL RECORD, DATA RECORDS, and STATUS RECORDS (see Figure 3.6).

For an IDoc used as a data package, the common analogy is a letter: the information on the sheet of paper corresponds to the data records, with business content; the envelope is the control record, which holds sender and receiver information (logical system names); and the status records are the additional processing information on the envelope—the stamp is franked, maybe the envelope is labeled "Delivery impossible, receiver unknown".

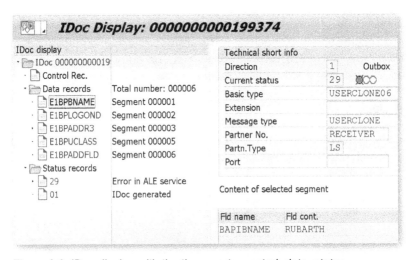

Figure 3.6: IDoc display with the three parts: control, data, status

You can select the individual data records to display the content on the right-hand side. In our example, we have only provided content for BA-PIBNAME (Figure 3.6 lower part), so there is nothing else to display.

The status records show two entries: the fact that the IDoc was generated (code 01), and an error in the ALE service (code 29).

Parts of the control record are already shown in the upper right part of the overview. We see the PARTNER NO. field (the receiver system) with the value *RECEIVER*, and the value *LS* for logical system in the PARTNER TYPE field. The field MESSAGE TYPE contains the value *USERCLONE*, and the field BASIC TYPE contains the value *USERCLONE06*. The message type is the classification of the business content and the basic type is the actual structure definition of the IDoc type, as explained in the next section.

Now let's see how easy it is to create the ALE interface objects for our own custom BAPI.

3.4   Creating BAPI ALE message types

If you have created a customer BAPI (which changes data in the target system), you may want to create the ALE message type so that you can send IDocs instead of a BAPI call to the target. This is also possible, with some restrictions as listed below.

To create the ALE message type, you use transaction BDBG. You can either start the transaction directly and enter the object type and method manually (*ZATHLETE* and *ZBAPICREATEFROMDATA*), or you can navigate there from the DETAIL view of your BAPI in transaction BAPI by double-clicking the entry *Does not exist* in the field ALE MESSAGE TYPE.

Use the first button CREATE ![button] to start the generation of the ALE message type. The first dialog box displays the proposal *Z_ATHLETE_ ZBAPICREATEFROMDATA* for the message type. Once you confirm this, the second dialog box displays the proposals for the IDoc type and the ALE modules (see Figure 3.7).

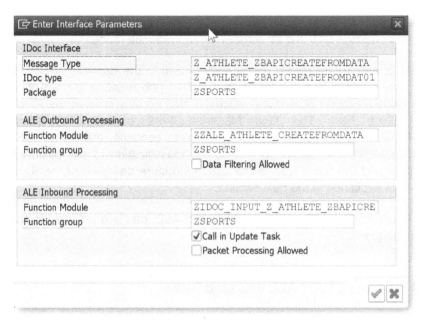

Figure 3.7: Proposal for ALE message type generation

Requirements for creating ALE message types

 There are certain requirements for creating the ALE message type for a BAPI. All interface parameters must reference data elements, not elementary types. Another requirement is that different interface parameters of the BAPI do not reference the same structure in the DDIC.

As an example, if our structure ZBAPIATHLETE referenced a prede-fined type for one of the fields (see Figure 2.22), then transaction BDBG would exit with the error DATA ELEMENT NOT ACTIVE.

In the ENTER INTERFACE PARAMETERS dialog box (Figure 3.7), press Enter to create the objects. The result is shown in Figure 3.8.

196

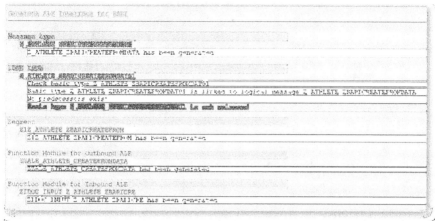

Figure 3.8: Generated objects for the ALE message type

Note the comment BASIC TYPE … IS NOT RELEASED. To release it, press
F3 to return to the initial screen of transaction BDBG and choose EDIT •
IDOC TYPE AND SEGMENT TYPE • RELEASE to release the type.

Message type, IDoc type, and basic type

The message type is just a name without details such as
structures or specific fields. It is used in the ALE
configuration. The actual structure is defined by an IDoc
type. All IDoc types belong to exactly one message type.
For a message type that is provided by SAP, there are
typically several IDoc types, as the interface has been extended over
the sequence of SAP releases. However, the message type has not
changed.

An IDoc type can be a basic type (defined by SAP or customers) or
an extended type. The latter is a customer extension of a basic type
which includes additional segments (structures).

We have now created our custom IDoc message type. We could now
start a test of the ALE outbound module again, but instead we will proceed to implement a complete scenario. It will include the required ALE
configuration to have the IDoc delivered to the target system and a report to create an IDoc. These two topics are covered in the following two
sections.

ALE message interface for any RFM

 Note that it is also possible to create an ALE message interface with transaction BDFG for any RFM—the module does not have to be a BAPI.

3.5   Setting up the ALE configuration

Logical systems

We have already mentioned the logical system briefly in Section 3.3, as part of the tip *ALE outbound module requires a logical system*. It is the first configuration object we will introduce. Others will follow step by step.

IDocs are data containers which are exchanged between two systems asynchronously. Both systems have to have a name assigned and the logical system name is used for this. Both the sender and receiver names are part of the IDoc data package.

For an ABAP system, each client is assigned a separate logical system name, as business data is client-specific. You use transaction BD54 to maintain the list of all logical system names that take part in the IDoc data exchange of that system—ABAP or non-ABAP.

The names of the logical systems have to be consistent throughout all the systems participating in the IDoc exchange—in our case: consistent in the client and target system. The client (or source) system is the system from which we send RFC requests to the server. We will name this client system CENTRAL. The server (or target) system contains the athletes' data in table ZATHLETE. The custom BAPI was initially defined there. This server system is called SPORTS.

We will define now the logical system names in both systems. Start transaction BD54, confirm the dialog box with the information that the table is cross-client, and maintain two new entries: logical system *SPORTS* with the name *Athlete data*, and logical system *CENTRAL* with the name *Central*. Save the entries. Repeat this in the other system so that both names are valid in both systems.

"Logical Systems" view is client-independent

 If your client (source) and server (target) systems are just different clients in the same ABAP system, you only maintain the logical system names once, as these can then be used in both systems.

We now assign a logical system name to the actual clients. Start transaction SCC4, select your ABAP client, and display the details. Check the attribute LOGICAL SYSTEM: if it is empty, maintain the value. Do this in both the client system using the value *CENTRAL* and in the server system using the value *SPORTS*.

Do not change existing logical system assignments

 If the clients already have logical system names assigned, it is a good idea not to change these, as they may already have been used by existing scenarios. In this case, make a mental note of the existing values; in the following steps, use these respective values instead of *CENTRAL* and *SPORTS*.

Logical system names are written to the IDoc data containers and changing the values may lead to inconsistencies in the system.

The configuration of the logical systems is **scenario-independent** in the sense that the systems can be used as a sender or a receiver or both for various interfaces.

Protocols for IDoc transmission

As already mentioned, IDocs can be transferred using different protocols. The choice of the protocol depends on the capabilities of the two systems involved.

For ABAP systems which are both sender and receiver, the protocol RFC is typically used. The sender system automatically uses an asynchronous technique such as tRFC or bgRFC. As usual, an RFC destination is required to deliver the IDoc. Keep in mind that if we use a report to generate the IDoc, we use a local call to the ALE outbound module and do not directly use the RFC destination.

ALE port in the client system

We already have the RFC destination FIRSTDEST in the client system, pointing to the target system. The next object is the port. An *ALE port* is a configuration object that defines the way the data is transferred; it specifies the protocol.

In our case, where we use the protocol RFC, the port is a kind of wrapper for the RFC destination. In the following ALE configuration, only the port is used. If the target system parameters change, the name of the RFC destination can be adapted inside the port but the ALE configuration as such (using the port name) remains unchanged.

Start transaction WE21 to display the overview PORTS IN IDOC PROCESSING. As you see here, several protocols can be used for the transition of an IDoc (shown in Figure 3.9, left-hand side). Select the protocol *Transactional RFC* and click the icon 📇 CREATE to create a new port. In the dialog box PORTS IN IDOC PROCESSING (not shown here), choose the option OWN PORT NAME and enter *SPORT_PORT*. Press Enter to proceed to the maintenance of the port. This is done on the right-hand side, as shown in Figure 3.9; the title of the screen has now changed to CREATING A TRFC PORT.

Maintain the DESCRIPTION field and enter *FIRSTDEST* in the RFC DESTINATION field. After you save the port, it is shown in the respective node on the left-hand side, as shown in Figure 3.9.

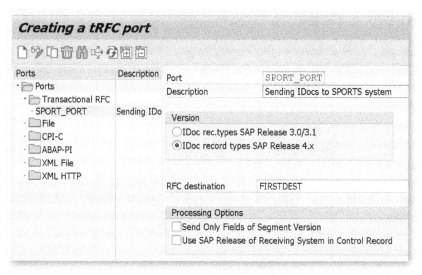

Figure 3.9: tRFC port maintained in transaction WE21

So far, our ALE configuration objects have been interface-independent. This will change with the next object, the partner profile. There, we configure specific interfaces: ALE message types and IDoc types.

Choice of scenario: ZATHLETE or USER

As mentioned in the tip ALE interfaces required in the source and target (Section 3.3), both sender and receiver systems need to have the ALE message type objects generated.

If you use separate systems (not simply different clients of the same system), you have probably defined the custom business object ZATHLETE with its BAPIs only in the target system so far.

The effort involved in creating first the business object with BAPI and then the associated ALE message type in the client system as well seems quite high. (Note that you can transport the ALE objects from within transaction BDBG, for example using the menu EDIT • TRANSPORT • OBJECTS IN OUTBOUND INTERFACE.) As an alternative, you can execute the following configuration with message type USERCLONE and IDoc type USERCLONE06 (shown in Figure 3.6).

Partner profile in the client system

This port is now used in the configuration object called *partner profile*. Start transaction WE20 to display the list of partner profiles. The different partner types show again the diversity of ALE, but our example focuses on logical systems only.

Therefore, select the node PARTNER TYPE LS and click the icon 🛅 CREATE. In the detail area on the right-hand side, enter *SPORTS* in the PARTNER NO. field. On the first tab, POST PROCESSING…, you have to enter data. Set the TYPE field to the value *US* (for user), maintain your user ID in the AGENT field, and maintain the LANGUAGE field, as shown in Figure 3.10.

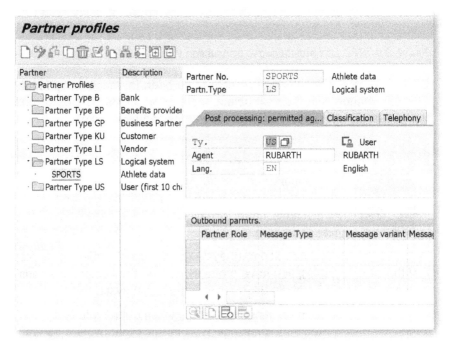

Figure 3.10: Creating a partner profile in the client

As soon as you save the partner profile, you can add an outbound parameter. Use the ![icon] icon below the table to do this. In the MESSAGE TYPE field,
maintain the ALE message type of the custom BAPI and in the RECEIVER
PORT field, choose the port *SPORT_PORT* that you have just created. You
can choose the IDoc type/basic type with the input help F4 .

Now select TRANSFER IDOCS IMMEDIATELY and press Enter . A new field
PACK. SIZE will appear, in which you enter *1*. Check your settings versus
Figure 3.11.

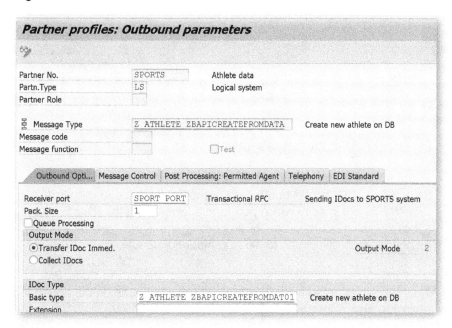

Figure 3.11: Outbound parameters for the partner profile in the client

Save the values and return to the overview of the partner profile. The
OUTBOUND PARAMETERS section now shows one line.

Figure 3.12 provides an overview of the required ALE configuration objects and their values for our scenario.

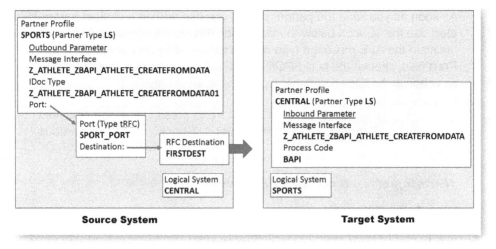

Figure 3.12: Overview of the ALE configuration objects for the scenario

Partner profile in the target system

In the target system, we have to configure how an incoming IDoc shall be handled. This is part of the partner profile, this time in the target system. We do not specify which port to use for sending the IDoc but we do specify which module to use for processing the IDoc. It will be a configuration that indirectly points to the ALE inbound module.

Start transaction WE20 in the target system, select the node PARTNER TYPE LS and click the icon 🗂 CREATE. In the detail area on the right-hand side, you now maintain the partner number as *CENTRAL*, as this is the sender of the IDoc. Apart from the partner number, the parameters should be as shown in Figure 3.10.

Now we maintain an inbound parameter. Use the respective icon 🗟 to create an inbound parameter (the button is only active after you save the partner profile).

Specify the message type again and maintain the process code as *BAPI* (see Figure 3.13). This will pass the incoming IDoc to the respective ALE inbound module belonging to the ALE interface of the BAPI.

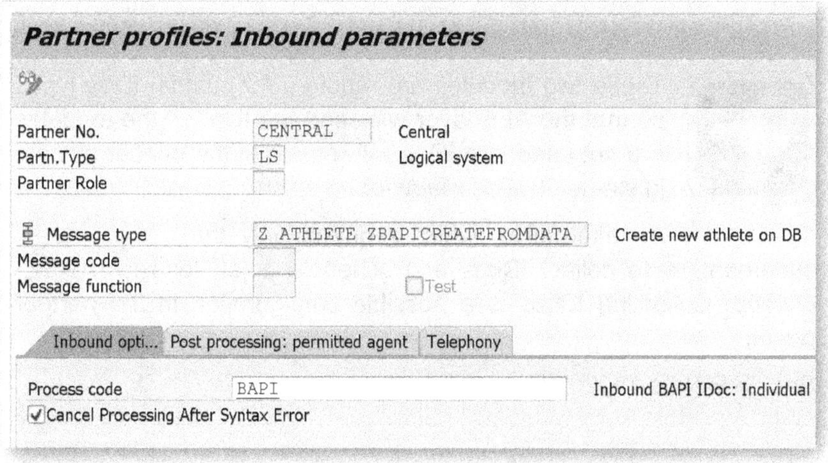

Partner profiles: Inbound parameters

Partner No.	CENTRAL	Central
Partn.Type	LS	Logical system
Partner Role		

☰ Message type	Z_ATHLETE ZBAPICREATEFROMDATA	Create new athlete on DB
Message code		
Message function		☐Test

Inbound opti... | Post processing: permitted agent | Telephony

Process code	BAPI	Inbound BAPI IDoc: Individual
✓Cancel Processing After Syntax Error		

Figure 3.13: Inbound parameters of the partner profile in the target

Now we should be set up for delivering the IDoc from the source to the target system. The next step is to create a report that creates an IDoc in the source system.

3.6 Sending an IDoc from a report

Instead of starting a single test for our ALE outbound module, we execute the module from within a report. The report must be created in the client system, with the logical system name CENTRAL.

We use parameters for the athlete data and for the receiver and a CALL FUNCTION statement on the ALE outbound module—a local call, as you already know.

There is an additional requirement: the COMMIT WORK statement is required, and it must be preceded by the call of the modules DB_COMMIT and DEQUEUE_ALL.

205

Modules DB_COMMIT and DEQUEUE_ALL

 These two modules are required for custom IDoc types so that the ALE layer will send the IDoc. If the modules are not used, the IDoc will remain in the sender system in status *30 IDoc ready for dispatch*.

An alternative, which requires only the COMMIT WORK statement, is to collect IDocs and schedule a job for report RSE-OUT00. Collecting IDocs is a possible configuration in the partner profile.

See SAP Note 150202 for details.

Additionally, we write the IDoc number as a result. We also show the IDoc status list (by means of IDOC_READ_COMPLETELY), which can be refreshed. Note that the design of the report with the statement AT LINE-SELECTION is rather ancient, but it offers an easy means of update, triggered by a user action.

An example of the report is shown below in Listing 3.1.

```
REPORT  z_create_idoc.

DATA: lt_receivers TYPE TABLE OF bdi_logsys,
      ls_receivers TYPE bdi_logsys,
      lt_documents TYPE TABLE OF swotobjid,
      ls_documents TYPE swotobjid,
      lt_edids TYPE TABLE OF edids,
      ls_edids TYPE edids,
      lv_name TYPE zbapiathlete-name,
      lv_bdate TYPE zbapiathlete-date_of_birth,
      lv_country TYPE zbapiathlete-country.

PARAMETERS: pa_nam(20) DEFAULT 'IDoc Athlete',
            pa_dat TYPE dats DEFAULT sy-datum,
            pa_cntry(2) DEFAULT 'GB',
            pa_logs type bdi_logsys-logsys default 'SPORTS'.

lv_name = pa_nam.
```

```
lv_bdate = pa_dat.
lv_country = pa_cntry.

ls_receivers-logsys = pa_logs.
APPEND ls_receivers TO lt_receivers.

CALL FUNCTION 'ZZALE_ATHLETE_CREATEFROMDATA'
   EXPORTING
     iathletename              = lv_name
     idateofbirth              = lv_bdate
     icountry                  = lv_country
     icountryiso               = ''
     itestrun                  = ''
*    OBJ_TYPE                  = 'ZATHLETE'
*    SERIAL_ID                 = '0'
   TABLES
     receivers                 = lt_receivers
     communication_documents   = lt_documents
*    APPLICATION_OBJECTS       =
   EXCEPTIONS
     error_creating_idocs      = 1
     OTHERS                    = 2.

IF sy-subrc <> 0.
   WRITE: 'Error during IDoc creation'.
   EXIT.
ENDIF.

CALL FUNCTION 'DB_COMMIT'.
CALL FUNCTION 'DEQUEUE_ALL'.
COMMIT WORK.
WRITE 'IDoc was provided for sending (click number to check stat
us)'.

LOOP AT lt_documents INTO ls_documents.
   WRITE: /, 'IDoc number:', ls_documents-objkey HOTSPOT.
ENDLOOP.

AT LINE-SELECTION.
   sy-lsind = 1. " Keeping list index
```

```
    ls_edids-docnum = ls_documents-objkey.

    CALL FUNCTION 'IDOC_READ_COMPLETELY'
      EXPORTING
        document_number              = ls_edids-docnum
*   IMPORTING
*     IDOC_CONTROL                   =
*     NUMBER_OF_DATA_RECORDS         =
*     NUMBER_OF_STATUS_RECORDS       =
      TABLES
        int_edids                    = lt_edids
*     INT_EDIDD                      =
    EXCEPTIONS
      document_not_exist             = 1
      document_number_invalid        = 2
      OTHERS                         = 3
          .
    IF sy-subrc <> 0.
      WRITE: 'Error ', sy-subrc, ' while checking IDoc status'.
    ENDIF.

    WRITE:  'Status of IDoc ', ls_documents-objkey.
    WRITE: / '(click here to refresh)' HOTSPOT.
    LOOP AT lt_edids INTO ls_edids.
      WRITE: / ls_edids-status, ls_edids-statxt, ls_edids-⌐
  stapa1, ls_edids-stapa2.
    ENDLOOP.
```

Listing 3.1: Report for creating an IDoc

Receiver specification

Note that we only specify one receiver. The sample coding is not able to reflect the situation of several IDocs that would be created in the case of several receivers.

ALE in general allows several receivers for a message. Later, we will learn how to configure receivers independent of any code.

Note that such a report should contain consistency checks, which we have skipped for now. Like the test for the module ALE_USER_CLONE in Section 3.3, we maintain one entry for table RECEIVERS with the value *SPORTS*.

ALE modules not remote-enabled

 You have probably already noticed that both ALE outbound and inbound modules are not remote-enabled. They are both for local execution only. We have already executed the ALE outbound module as a test, and you may have created the report for this.

The ALE inbound module in the target system will not be executed directly from the client via RFC. Instead, each ABAP system has a generic entry point (an RFM) that receives all IDocs, regardless of their ALE message type. In addition, protocols other than RFC are possible for the transmission of an IDoc, as discussed in Section 3.5.

Execute the report and check the IDoc status. If the ALE configuration is set up correctly, you should no longer receive the error message ERROR IN ALE SERVICE.

In addition, use the status monitor for ALE messages (transaction BD87) to display the details of the IDoc. Compared to the first IDoc we created (Figure 3.6), we see just one segment on the left-hand side, containing the athlete's data. But which athlete number was assigned to the new athlete in the target system?

Log on to the target system and use transaction BD87 to check for the IDoc in the target. You will see that the target system has assigned a new IDoc number which is different to that in the source system. The IDoc status information is also different, so it is valid only locally.

Figure 3.14 shows a green status code for the success: APPLICATION DOCUMENT POSTED, and even the athlete number is shown.

Status Monitor for ALE Messages

🔁 ⊞ 🗐 ▀ ⬚ 🎏 Select IDocs   &⁈Display IDocs   ⮕Trace IDocs   ⓟProcess

IDocs	IDoc Status	Number
· 🎏 IDoc selection		
· ▀ Athlete data		0
· ⮔ IDocs in outbound processing		0
· ⮔ IDoc in inbound processing		1
· ☐ Application document posted	53	1
· ⬚ Z_ATHLETE_ZBAPICREATEFROMDATA		1
· i ZSPORTS(000) : & & & &		1
· i New athlete was stored 000000000115		1

Figure 3.14: IDoc status in the target shows the athlete number created

How about having this information in the source system as well? This is not possible, you will say, as we have discussed that asynchronous techniques do not deliver a business response and IDocs are always transferred asynchronously.

Well, that is true for the interface: the **interface** does not provide an immediate business response for asynchronous techniques. However, the overall **process** may cover more than one interface. Consider that the business process can cover two interfaces, both asynchronous.

The first interface is used for the transmission of the data from the client to the server, as we have already done. The second interface is used for the transmission back to the initial client, providing information about the status of the data sent. This status information sent back to the initial sender at a later point in time is often called an *acknowledgement*. This situation is illustrated in Figure 3.15.

It is possible to provide this type of acknowledgement for ALE technology—it just requires additional configuration. Therefore, we will discuss ALE configuration further in the next section. Some configuration objects that we have already used are relevant and a new one will be introduced.

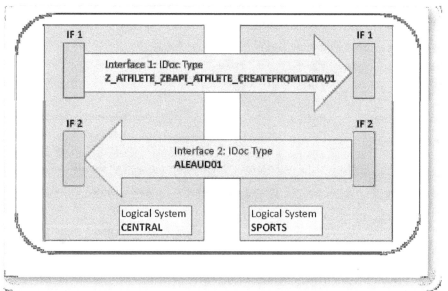

Figure 3.15: Business process with two asynchronous interfaces

3.7 Configuring ALE audit responses

The configuration of an ALE acknowledgement is based on the message interface ALEAUD. We have to enable the route from the target system back to the source system. In our case, we have to configure a partner profile in SPORTS that references an RFC destination from SPORTS to CENTRAL.

In the target system SPORTS, use transaction WE20 to create a partner profile for partner number *CENTRAL*. In the OUTBOUND PARAMETERS section, create a new entry, specifying message type *ALEAUD* and IDoc type *ALEAUD01*. Reference a new port of type *Transactional RFC* (transaction WE21) like in Figure 3.9, which in turn references a new RFC destination (see Figure 1.3). As before, set the PACKAGE SIZE field to *1* and select TRANSFER IDOC IMMED. Compare your settings with Figure 3.16.

211

Partner profiles: Outbound parameters

Partner No.   CENTRAL   Central
Partn.Type   LS   Logical system
Partner Role

Message Type   ALEAUD   ALE: Confirmations for Inbound IDocs
Message code
Message function   ☐Test

| Outbound Opti... | Message Control | Post Processing: Permitted Agent | Telephony | EDI Standard |

Receiver port   CENTRAL AD   Transactional RFC   Send ALEAUD back to central
Pack. Size   1
☐Queue Processing
Output Mode
◉Transfer IDoc Immed.   Output Mode   2
◯Collect IDocs

IDoc Type
Basic type   ALEAUD01   Confirmations of the processing sta.
Extension
View
☑Cancel Processing After Syntax Error
Seg. release in IDoc type   Segment Appl. Rel.

Figure 3.16: Outbound partner profile in SPORTS for ALEAUD

This defines the route back to CENTRAL.

Now, in the CENTRAL system, we have to define the required activity for this incoming IDoc. Therefore, we define a partner profile with inbound parameters for *ALEAUD*, with process code *AUD1* (see Figure 3.17).

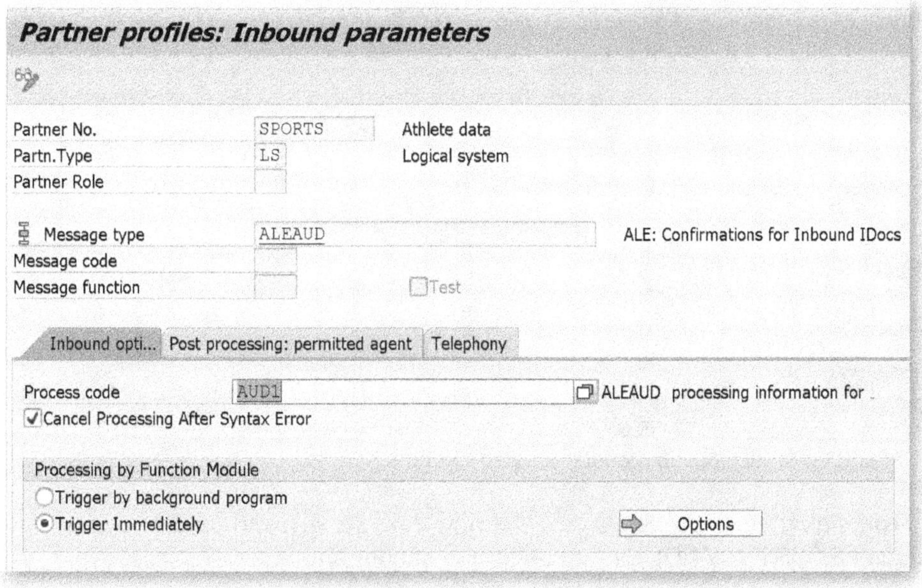

Partner profiles: Inbound parameters

Partner No.	SPORTS	Athlete data	
Partn.Type	LS	Logical system	
Partner Role			

Message type	ALEAUD		ALE: Confirmations for Inbound IDocs
Message code			
Message function		☐Test	

Inbound opti... | Post processing: permitted agent | Telephony

Process code AUD1 ☐ ALEAUD processing information for
☑Cancel Processing After Syntax Error

Processing by Function Module
○Trigger by background program
◉Trigger Immediately   ⇨   Options

Figure 3.17: Inbound partner profile in CENTRAL for ALEAUD

We already know these configuration objects but from the other perspective. For ALEAUD, however, an additional configuration is required. In
the target system, we have to define which systems should receive an
ALEAUD as acknowledgement. We do this with the *distribution model*.

The ALE distribution model is a central place for modeling scenarios. It
groups message types by the sender and the receiver logical systems.
And for some ALE functionality, it is a requirement to have such a model
as configuration. This is the case, for example, for the master data distribution of material data—and for ALEAUD messages.

Start the distribution model overview in target system SPORTS via
transaction BD64. You will probably see a list of existing models that we
are not focusing on. Create your own model by clicking CREATE MODEL
VIEW (see the upper part of Figure 3.18). Note that the lower part of the
figure already shows the state after the next step.

213

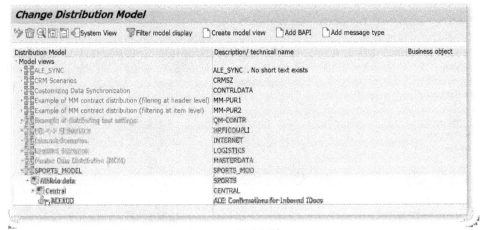

Figure 3.18: Distribution model view in SPORTS

The dialog box ADD MESSAGE TYPE now asks for a name for the model (use *SPORTS_MOD*), as well as for the sender and receiver logical system names and the message type. Provide the respective values, as shown in Figure 3.19.

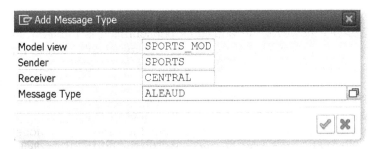

Figure 3.19: Creating a new model view for ALEAUD

Save the distribution model. It now includes your model view, as was already visible in the lower part of Figure 3.18.

The last part of the configuration is a batch job for report RBDSTATE, which will trigger the creation of the ALEAUD IDocs periodically.

Job scheduling required for ALEAUD

 You have to schedule a recurring batch job for report RBDSTATE in the target system SPORTS. The report variant must include the sender system that will receive the ALEAUD IDoc (parameter CONFIRMATIONS FOR SYSTEM)—for our scenario this is CENTRAL.

Instead of a batch job (or if you are not patient enough to wait for the next job run), you can start the report manually in the target system after you have sent the IDoc from the client system, using the report Z_CREATE_IDOC.

You can check the details of an ALEAUD IDoc in the target system SPORTS. In the DATA RECORDS area, the second structure *E1STATE* (*Segment 000002*) will show the reference to the initial IDoc number (*DOCNUM*) and the athlete number (*STAPA2_LNG*), as shown in Figure 3.20.

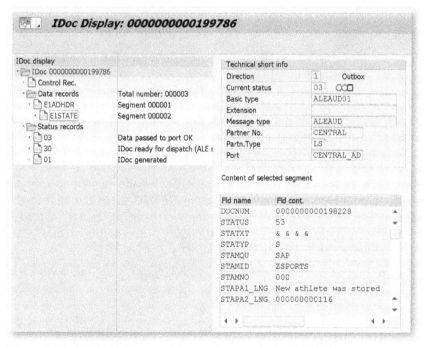

Figure 3.20: ALEAUD IDoc contains a reference to the initial IDoc

If the ALEAUD IDoc remains in the status *30 IDoc ready for dispatch* in the target system SPORTS, you may have to run report RSEOUT00. We mentioned this report at the beginning of Section 3.6, in the tip *Modules DB_COMMIT and DEQUEUE_ALL*.

With this ALE acknowledgement configuration based on ALEAUD, the report Z_CREATE_IDOC will now show the number of the new athlete—created in the target—even in the client. And if you send incorrect data (for example, country value *YY*), the error message INVALID DATA is shown in the source system as well after a few minutes.

Importance of the distribution model

 In our explanations, we have only used the distribution model with a model view for the ALEAUD configuration. However, the distribution model is a very central and important configuration point for various ALE scenarios.

Typically, you do not maintain a receiver in a report directly; instead, you maintain potential receiver systems in the distribution model. A lot of scenarios delivered by SAP presume that the distribution roles are maintained in the distribution model.

The distribution model offers advanced features like generation of partner profiles and distribution of model views across systems.

Let us appreciate the importance of the distribution model now in our report as well. The report will enable an IDoc to be sent even without a receiver being specified in the report.

Maintain a new model view BAPI_MODEL for the distribution model (transaction BD64) in our sender system CENTRAL. In contrast to the approach for our first model view (where we used the button ADD MESSAGE TYPE), we now use the button ADD BAPI. The sender is *CENTRAL*, the receiver is *SPORTS*, the object name is *Z_ATHLETE*, and the method is *ZbapiCreatefromdata*. Compare your settings with Figure 3.21 and save the distribution model.

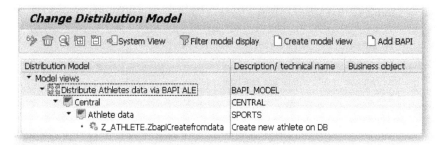

Figure 3.21: Model view in sender CENTRAL for BAPI via ALE

In our report Z_CREATE_IDOC, we extend the part at which we have added the receiver to the internal table. If no logical system is provided on the selection screen, the report checks whether a receiver is maintained in the distribution model. We use a local call to module ALE_ASYNC_BAPI_GET_RECEIVER for this. The module expects the business object type and the method name. Note that this module is only used to check model views for BAPIs, and not for ALE message types—we will discuss these later.

Listing 3.2 is an example for the proposed extension.

```
DATA: lt_filterobject_values type table of BDI_FOBJ.
...
lv_country = pa_cntry.

IF pa_logs IS NOT INITIAL.
  ls_receivers-logsys = pa_logs.
  APPEND ls_receivers TO lt_receivers.
  WRITE: 'Receiver manually set: ', pa_logs.
ELSE.
*Data: lt_filterobject_values TYPE TABLE OF  bdi_fobj.
  CALL FUNCTION 'ALE_ASYNC_BAPI_GET_RECEIVER'
    EXPORTING
      object                 = 'ZATHLETE'
      method                 = 'ZBAPICREATEFROMDATA'
    TABLES
*     RECEIVER_INPUT         =
      receivers              = lt_receivers
      filterobject_values    = lt_filterobject_values
    EXCEPTIONS
```

```
          error_in_filterobjects    = 1
          error_in_ale_customizing  = 2
          OTHERS                     = 3.
   IF sy-subrc <> 0.
     WRITE: 'Error during receiver check: ', sy-subrc.
     EXIT.
   ELSE.
     DESCRIBE TABLE lt_receivers.
     IF sy-tfill IS INITIAL.
       WRITE: 'No receiver in Distribution Model'.
       EXIT.
     ELSE.
       LOOP AT lt_receivers INTO ls_receivers.
         WRITE: / 'Receiver from Model view:',
                   ls_receivers-logsys.
       ENDLOOP.
     ENDIF.
   ENDIF.
ENDIF.

CALL FUNCTION 'ZZALE_ATHLETE_CREATEFROMDATA'
...
```

Listing 3.2: Extending report Z_CREATE_IDOC to check the receiver

This ends the excursus on the business process using two interfaces. The advantage of ALE is that you can set up such an acknowledgement easily and out of the box. There is no need to create a specific RFM in the target that provides the status of the data initially sent.

So far, we have focused on the BAPI ALE interface. Now we will broaden the discussion to the general ALE approach, using any ALE message type. Nevertheless, we will stick to the development aspects: even for a message type without a BAPI relation, you can create a respective IDoc using ABAP statements. Instead of using the ALE outbound module (which is part of the specific BAPI ALE interface), we use the generic module MASTER_IDOC_DISTRIBUTE.

3.8 Creating IDocs generic

The generic module MASTER_IDOC_DISTRIBUTE allows you to create an IDoc for any ALE message type. We will use this now in a new report and learn more about the IDoc structure parts: control record, data records, and status records.

Analyzing the ALE outbound module

 Check the source code of the ALE outbound module ZZA-LE_ATHLETE_CREATEFROMDATA that we used previously. You will see the call for ALE_IDOCS _CREATE. Open this module by forward navigation (double-click the name). The short text in the module's attribute is *Replacement for MASTER_IDOC_DISTRIBUTE for asynchronous BAPIs*. This shows the relationship between the two modules.

Following the approach of the distribution model as the central place for receiver configuration, we will not specify a receiver in our report directly. Instead, we use the module ALE_MODEL_INFO_GET to check for an existing receiver. This module checks maintained **message types**—in contrast to the module ALE_ASYNC_BAPI_GET_RECEIVER, which we used to check for maintained **BAPI message types**.

Our scenario is now using material master data again. In Section 2.5, we have already used the respective BAPI. Now we use the message type MATMAS with IDoc type MATMAS03.

Message type and IDoc type relation

 You can use transaction WE82 to see the correlation of message type to IDoc types. IDoc types have been adapted over time, with new fields added, thus we have a kind of counter as a suffix.

The concept allows you to use one message type in the distribution model for several receivers but use different IDoc types for each receiver in the partner profiles. For example, for a target system with a lower release, the partner profile will reference an older IDoc type supported in that release.

Use transaction WE30 to check the details of IDoc type MATMAS03. On the initial screen, enter *MATMAS03* as the object name and click DISPLAY to see the details.

The structures (called segments) are listed in a hierarchy. Double-click the first segment *E1MARAM* to see the information for the segment, as shown in Figure 3.22.

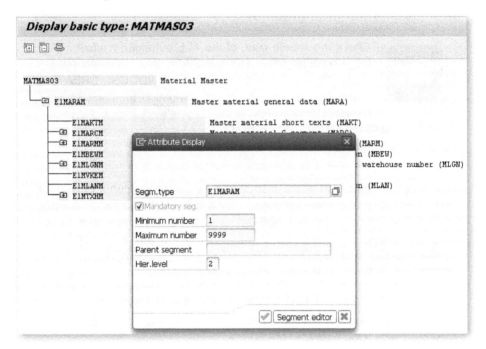

Figure 3.22: MATMAS segments with E1MARAM attributes

To see the fields of the segment with their details, click SEGMENT EDITOR (the result is not shown here).

The second segment we use is *E1MAKTM* for the short texts. It is mandatory, as is *E1MARAM* in Figure 3.22. Check the fields of this segment using the segment editor as well. The other segments are optional.

The question now is which fields of the IDoc data records do we have to maintain? For the BAPI call, we have used the required fields in the respective report shown in Listing 2.5. Unfortunately, the fields for the IDoc type have different names to those in the BAPI structure.

You can use transaction WE60 to display the IDoc type documentation in HTML format. The search for the string *sector*, for example, will show the field E1MARAM-MBRSH, which correlates to the BAPI field BAPI-MATHEAD-IND_SECTOR. The other correlations are MATL_TYPE -> MTART, BASE_UOM -> MEINS, BASIC_VIEW -> WRKST.

The module MASTER_IDOC_DISTRIBUTE imports the control record structure which references structure EDIDC (suffix C for control record). In the TABLES section of the module, we find references to EDIDS (S for status record) and EDIDD (D for data record). Note that all these structures are **generic** structures, in contrast to the **application-specific** segments of MATMAS03, like E1MARAM. We will therefore fill the application data in the segments and then embed this segment into the generic structure EDIDD.

Field EDIDD-SDATA contains all application data

 Field SDATA is the field of structure EDIDD which contains all the application data of one segment. For each segment, a separate row is used in EDIDD. The application data is serialized in field SDATA without a delimiter. EDIDD includes field SEGNAM, so the structure somehow delivers the *mask* for the de-serialization of the data chain in SDATA.

We have not seen the field SDATA so far when checking IDoc content, for example in Figure 3.20, because monitor transactions such as BD87 already format the application data accordingly. You can check the field SDATA later when you run the report, using the debugger.

In our report, we use structure LS_EDIDC to pass the message type and the IDoc type to the module. Internal table LT_EDIDD is used to pass the data of the material to the module. And internal table LT_EDIDC is used after the call to retrieve the IDoc number. Check Listing 3.3 as a proposal:

```
REPORT  z_create_matmas.

DATA: lt_edids TYPE TABLE OF edids,
      ls_edids TYPE edids,
      lt_edidc TYPE TABLE OF edidc,
      ls_edidc TYPE edidc,
      lt_edidd TYPE TABLE OF edidd,
      ls_edidd TYPE edidd,
      ls_header TYPE e1maram,
      ls_texts TYPE e1maktm.

PARAMETERS: pa_matnr(18) default 'IDOCMAT123'.

CALL FUNCTION 'ALE_MODEL_INFO_GET'
   EXPORTING
     message_type                = 'MATMAS'
*    RECEIVING_SYSTEM            = ' '
*    SENDING_SYSTEM             = ' '
*    VALIDDATE                  = SY-DATUM
*  TABLES
*    MODEL_DATA                 =
   EXCEPTIONS
     no_model_info_found         = 1
     own_system_not_defined      = 2
     OTHERS                      = 3
             .
IF sy-subrc <> 0.
   WRITE: 'Exception during model retrieve:', sy-subrc.
   EXIT.
ENDIF.

* control record
ls_edidc-mestyp = 'MATMAS'.
ls_edidc-idoctp = 'MATMAS03'.
```

```
* data record
*E1MARAM: general data
ls_edidd-segnum = 1. " first segment
ls_edidd-psgnum = 0. " no parent segment
ls_edidd-segnam = 'E1MARAM'. " see WE30

ls_header-matnr = pa_matnr.
ls_header-mbrsh = 'M'.
ls_header-mtart = 'FERT'.
ls_header-meins = 'EA'.
ls_header-wrkst = 'X'.

ls_edidd-sdata = ls_header.
append ls_edidd to lt_edidd.

*E1MAKTM: short texts
ls_edidd-segnum = 2. "second segment
ls_edidd-psgnum = 1. " parent is E1MARAM
ls_edidd-segnam = 'E1MAKTM'.

ls_texts-spras = 'EN'.
ls_texts-maktx = 'IDoc material'.
ls_edidd-sdata = ls_texts.
append ls_edidd to lt_edidd.

ls_edidd-segnum = 3. "third segment
ls_edidd-psgnum = 1. " parent is E1MARAM
ls_edidd-segnam = 'E1MAKTM'.

ls_texts-spras = 'DE'.
ls_texts-maktx = 'IDoc Material'.
ls_edidd-sdata = ls_texts.
append ls_edidd to lt_edidd.

CALL FUNCTION 'MASTER_IDOC_DISTRIBUTE'
  EXPORTING
    master_idoc_control           = ls_edidc
*   OBJ_TYPE                      = ''
*   CHNUM                         = ''
```

```
    TABLES
      communication_idoc_control    = lt_edidc
      master_idoc_data              = lt_edidd
    EXCEPTIONS
      error_in_idoc_control         = 1
      error_writing_idoc_status     = 2
      error_in_idoc_data            = 3
      sending_logical_system_unknown = 4
      OTHERS                        = 5.
IF sy-subrc <> 0.
  WRITE: 'Error in master IDoc distribute ', sy-subrc.
ENDIF.

CALL FUNCTION 'DB_COMMIT'.
CALL FUNCTION 'DEQUEUE_ALL'.
COMMIT WORK.
WRITE 'IDoc was provided for sending (click number to check ⏎
status)'.

LOOP AT lt_edidc INTO ls_edidc.
  WRITE: /, 'IDoc number:', ls_edidc-docnum HOTSPOT.
ENDLOOP.

AT LINE-SELECTION.
  sy-lsind = 1. " Keeping list index


  CALL FUNCTION 'IDOC_READ_COMPLETELY'
    EXPORTING
      document_number              = ls_edidc-docnum
*  IMPORTING
*    IDOC_CONTROL                  =
*    NUMBER_OF_DATA_RECORDS        =
*    NUMBER_OF_STATUS_RECORDS      =
    TABLES
      int_edids                    = lt_edids
*    INT_EDIDD                     =
  EXCEPTIONS
```

```
document_not_exist            = 1
document_number_invalid       = 2
OTHERS                        = 3
        .
IF sy-subrc <> 0.
   WRITE: 'Error ', sy-subrc, ' while checking IDoc status'.
ENDIF.

WRITE:  'Status of IDoc ', ls_edidc-docnum.
WRITE: / '(click here to refresh)' HOTSPOT.
LOOP AT lt_edids INTO ls_edids.
   WRITE: / ls_edids-status, ls_edids-statxt, ls_edids-⤶
stapa1, ls_edids-stapa2.
   ENDLOOP.
```

Listing 3.3: Report for creating a MATMAS03 IDoc

Master IDoc and communication IDocs

The *master IDoc* contains the data provided by the report and is a kind of template. For each configured receiver, a separate *communication IDoc* is created. As the IDoc type can be specific for each receiver, the communication IDocs may be slightly different.

You can test this later by maintaining two receiver systems and specifying different IDoc types (e.g., MATMAS01 and MATMAS03) in the partner profiles.

The required configuration for the scenario is the same as before but now we use a different port type:

▶ Extend the model view (CENTRAL-> SPORTS) with MATMAS

▶ Create a new ALE port of type FILE

▶ Extend the partner profile with a new outbound parameter for MATMAS/MATMAS03, referencing the FILE port

225

The FILE port is easy to configure. Figure 3.23 shows an example.

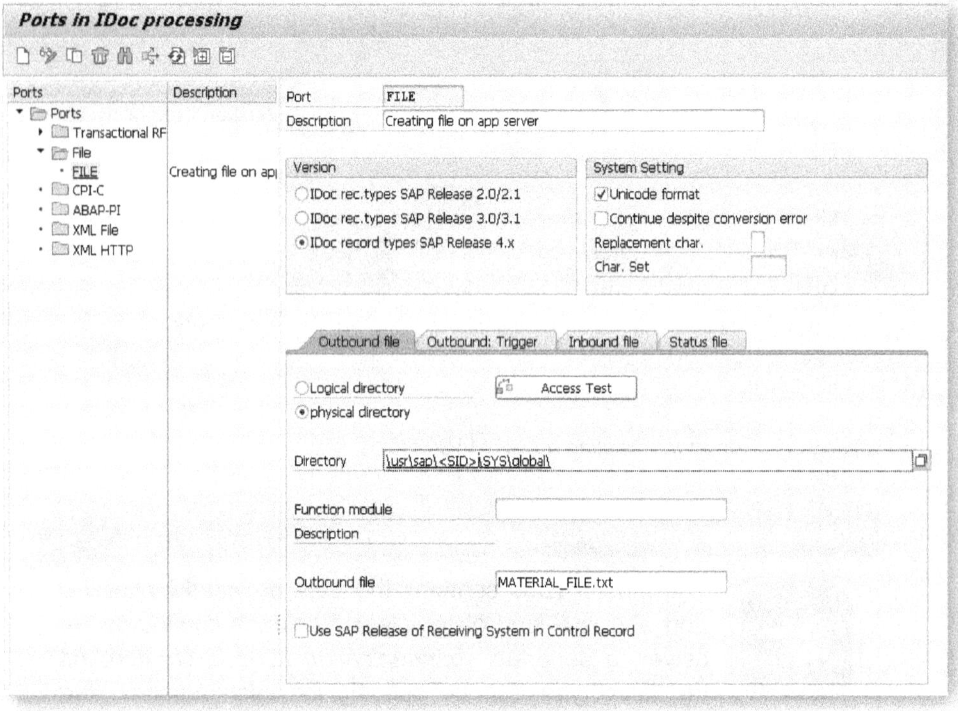

Figure 3.23: ALE File port (<SID> is a placeholder for your SID)

Note that the value in the DIRECTORY field contains a placeholder just for the screenshot—this will not work as a value. Nevertheless, it is possible to use a module to generate a specific file name.

The port is then used in the existing partner profile for the logical system SPORTS but in an additional outbound parameter for message type MATMAS. Figure 3.24 shows the outbound parameters.

Now you can start the report and check the IDoc status. Status 03 will show *IDoc written to file* if the configuration is correct.

The only thing left to discuss now is the usual ALE overview that focuses only on configuration and not on development. We will discuss this in the following section.

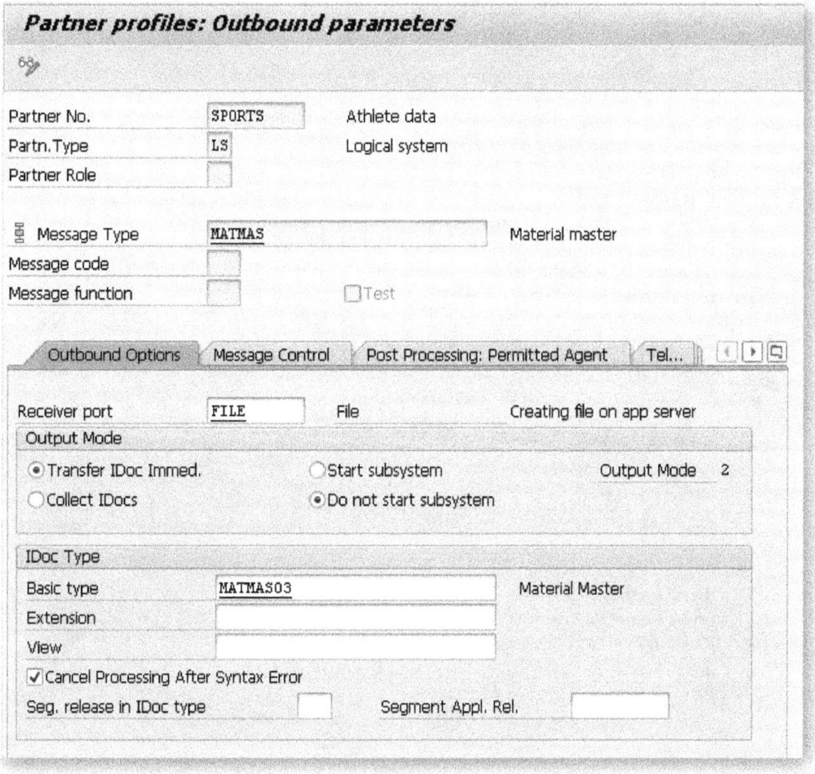

Partner profiles: Outbound parameters

Partner No.	SPORTS	Athlete data	
Partn.Type	LS	Logical system	
Partner Role			

Message Type	MATMAS	Material master	
Message code			
Message function		☐Test	

| Outbound Options | Message Control | Post Processing: Permitted Agent | Tel... |

Receiver port   FILE   File   Creating file on app server

Output Mode
- ⦿ Transfer IDoc Immed.   ◯ Start subsystem   Output Mode   2
- ◯ Collect IDocs   ⦿ Do not start subsystem

IDoc Type

Basic type	MATMAS03	Material Master	
Extension			
View			

☑ Cancel Processing After Syntax Error

Seg. release in IDoc type   Segment Appl. Rel.

Figure 3.24: Partner profile outbound parameters for MATMAS

3.9   Finding ALE options

ALE (Application Link Enabling) offers a broad variety of scenarios that can be implemented without any development effort. SAP provides all the required objects and transactions and you just have to configure the scenario following the *Implementation Guide (IMG)*. The scenarios are listed there and the relevant transactions are linked.

For the *ALE configuration*, you can use transaction SALE, which shows the respective ALE part of the IMG only. You will find several known objects listed there, see Figure 3.25.

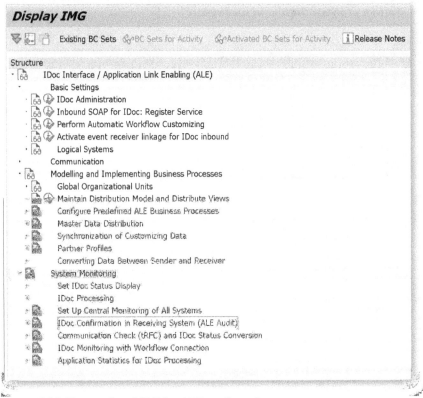

Figure 3.25: Transaction SALE for ALE configurations

ALE protocols

As already mentioned, you can use various port types for IDoc processing. In addition to the tRFC which we used, bgRFC and SOAP are also options. For bgRFC, consider transaction WE20BGRFC. For SOAP, Figure 3.25 above shows the entry INBOUND SOAP FOR IDOC.

In general, it is possible to distribute master data as well as transactional data between SAP and even non-SAP systems. An example is the master data distribution for materials. You set up a new model view in the distribution model, configure the partner profiles and ports, and you enable the change pointer. The change pointer will detect any change in the system, such as a new material creation, and will send this material to the respective systems as an IDoc, following the paths defined in the distribution model.

ALE and EDI

 The ALE concept of IDocs as data containers is similar to the concept used in Electronic Data Interchange (EDI). A clear separation of these terms is hard to find and will probably not be relevant for your work.

Typically, you can say that with ALE, you exchange one data package as it is—typically master data.

With EDI, a middleware between the sender and receiver will transfer the data package provided by the sender (e.g., a customer creates a purchase order) to a data package with a different structure for the receiver (e.g., supplier receives an order).

We have now highlighted the main aspects of IDocs and ALE that are important for an ABAP developer. We have seen that this technology offers a lot of content delivered by SAP: from interface definition through configuration to monitoring.

Now we will do a side step and have quick look at another area of SAP interfaces: the SAP Connectors.

4 SAP Connectors

Up to this point, we have discussed rather "classical" SAP interface technology which is proprietary. In former times, especially when ABAP systems did not support open standards like HTTP on their own, SAP introduced SAP Connectors as a kind of middleware, allowing non-SAP systems to connect to ABAP systems. Nowadays, ABAP speaks Internet: the application server supports Internet protocols without the need for additional middleware.

This book is aimed at ABAP developers and SAP Connectors do not contain or require any ABAP implementation.

However, it is helpful to know which connectors exist and which approach they follow so that for any project that involves external communication interfaces, you can decide whether connectors should be involved. The previous chapters have covered the ABAP aspects of such a project.

To get an overview of the connectors that SAP offers, use the quick link *https://support.sap.com/connectors* in SAP Support Portal. Figure 4.1 shows the first part of this page.

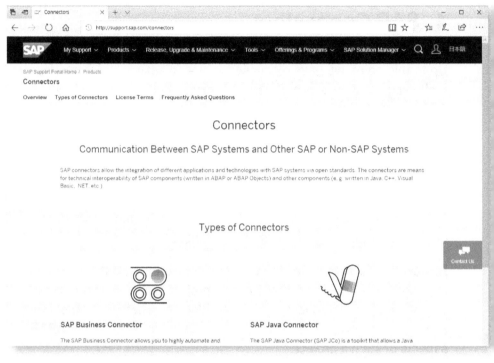

Figure 4.1: List of SAP Connectors in SAP Support Portal

4.1   SAP Business Connector

The *SAP Business Connector* is a standalone java application with its own web server integrated. It uses the RFC protocol to enable RFM, BAPIs, and IDoc communication in both directions (outbound and inbound). It allows the creation of services that connect to an ABAP system and/or any web resource. You can implement these services in Java coding or in a *flow* that is modelled using a graphical user interface.

SAP Business Connector is a lightweight and flexible connector that allows you to establish communication between different kinds of systems without any coding. Its main aspect is the conversion between RFC and HTTP at protocol level, as well as mapping between different structures. SAP Business Connector supports synchronous as well as asynchronous communication. Therefore, you can create a service that receives data via HTTP and converts this data into an ABAP format. This data can be used to send an IDoc to the ABAP system or to call an RFM/BAPI, either synchronously or asynchronously.

SAP Business Connector uses the SAP Java Connector

 The SAP Business Connector is a java application that in turn uses the SAP Java Connector for the RFC communication with the ABAP system. The SAP Java Connector is delivered as part of the SAP Business Connector installation.

4.2 SAP Java Connector

The *SAP Java Connector (JCo)* is a JNI-based RFC middleware that allows you to develop Java applications for communication to ABAP systems. It supports RFM, BAPI, and IDoc communication in both directions (outbound and inbound). JCo offers an easy-to-use API for all aspects such as connection pooling, metadata storage, and much more. It supports synchronous as well as asynchronous communication.

Furthermore, JCo is an integrated part of each dual-stack system (ABAP and Java stack) and enables the communication between ABAP and Java as an integrated SAP Resource Adapter.

IDoc support via Java IDocLibrary

 For handling IDocs, the IDocLibrary provided by SAP allows you to create, receive, and modify IDocs prior to sending or receiving the IDoc.

4.3 SAP NetWeaver RFC library

The *SAP NetWeaver RFC Library* offers a C/C++ interface for connecting to ABAP systems. It allows any development language that is capable to access such a library to enable communication with an ABAP system, in both directions (outbound and inbound). It supports synchronous as well as asynchronous communication. The library does not offer specific support for the use of IDoc structures.

The library is part of the kernel for the respective platform. The section on *http://service.sap.com/connectors* about the SAP NetWeaver RFC library references the respective SAP Notes for information on how to download the latest version of the library. Or you can simply search the download area for the string "SAP NW RFC SDK".

On Windows operating systems, you should add the path of the nwrfcsdk/lib folder to the PATH environment variable.

The library archive is delivered with demo programs as well as two compiled executables: rfcexec.exe and startrfc.exe. Before using them, you should consider the security settings in your ABAP system, especially the secinfo file for the SAP Gateway.

Incompatibility to former RFC library

 The *RFC library* is the predecessor of the SAP NetWeaver RFC library. Applications developed with the old RFC library must be adapted due to incompatible changes in the library.

The demo executable startrfc.exe no longer allows you to execute any RFM; it is now restricted to two EDI-related modules. Use `startrfc.exe -?` to see the details of the usage.

The demo executable rfcexec.exe acts as a mediator for outgoing calls from ABAP. You start it with parameters specifying the gateway on which it should register, using a dedicated program ID as the external partner:

```
rfcexec -a PROG_ID -g <hostname> -x <sysnr>
```

You must consider the security settings on the gateway—they may not allow external programs to connect to the gateway.

You can display this registration in the Gateway Monitor by choosing GOTO • LOGGED ON CLIENTS (although the external programs act as an RFC **server**, not **client**). The system type will show as *Registered Server*.

4.4   SAP Connector for Microsoft .NET

The *SAP Connector for Microsoft .NET* is an RFC middleware that allows you to develop .NET applications (like C#) for communication to ABAP systems. It supports RFM, BAPI, and IDoc communication in both directions (outbound and inbound). The connector has implemented the RFC protocol in C#, so there is no reference to the SAP NetWeaver RFC library. Just like with the SAP NetWeaver RFC Library, the SAP Connector for Microsoft .NET does not offer specific support for handling IDocs.

5 RFM und BAPIs in SAP S/4HANA

SAP S/4HANA is ABAP-based, so function modules can also be used for interface programming—both within the system and from outside. This chapter explains important aspects of using function modules in SAP S/4HANA.

5.1 Introducing SAP S/4HANA

SAP S/4HANA is "a real-time enterprise resource management suite for digital business", as stated on the official SAP web page. It is a new product line and not the successor to SAP ERP. The long name of the product is *SAP Business Suite 4 SAP HANA*.

Suite-on-HANA versus Suite-4-HANA

 The unofficial, but common phrase *Suite-on-HANA (SoH)* is used for an SAP system that runs on the *SAP HANA database*, for example *SAP ERP on SAP HANA*. As you know, *SAP ERP* is also supported to run on different database types.

This is not the case for SAP S/4HANA: this product line runs only on the SAP HANA database.

Nevertheless, some components are just like they are in SAP ERP, on component level as well as object level. SAP S/4HANA is also based on ABAP software components, and we will find SAP_BASIS just like in SAP ERP—but not SAP_APPL.

When talking about SAP S/4HANA, it is important to clarify whether we are talking about the on-premise edition or the cloud edition. As we are discussing custom development in this book, it is relevant to mention that custom development is not allowed in *SAP S/4HANA cloud*.

Simplification in SAP S/4HANA

With a product running on SAP HANA database exclusively, the full potential of this database can be used. The transition to this new product was used to simplify several aspects, such as processes and functionalities, and these simplifications are described in the *Simplification List*.

Simplification List

 The Simplification List explains all aspects that have changed in SAP S/4HANA compared to SAP ERP. These include business aspects such as solutions and features, but also technical aspects such as interfaces.

You can find the simplification list at *http://help.sap.com/s4hana* and then by navigating to the respective SAP S/4HANA product version.

One important aspect of simplification is that the data model has changed, also at database level. With SAP HANA as the database, it is possible to compute results on the fly, so there is no need for aggregate tables. And the new data model comes with new tables: table MATDOC, for example, replaces a lot of old logistics tables.

Another aspect of simplification is that some business functionalities or technical features have been changed or deprecated. This simplifies the usage of the functionalities and features and eliminates concurring techniques with overlapping features.

As an example, the *Warehouse Management* (LE-WM) is no longer the *target architecture* within SAP S/4HANA. Instead, you should use *Extended Warehouse Management* (SAP EWM). The term *target architecture* refers to the situation in which several technologies exist in parallel and SAP is investing only in some of them.

5.2 Using interfaces in SAP S/4HANA

If SAP S/4HANA consists of ABAP software components, we can therefore assume that RFC as protocol and RFMs and BAPIs as interfaces are supported. That is true, and we can use our knowledge on these topics in SAP S/4HANA as well.

The statement from SAP is that RFM/BAPI and ALE/IDoc development is not part of the SAP S/4HANA target architecture of SAP S/4HANA. Nevertheless, we can be sure that these technologies will not fade out within a couple of years.

What about the RFM and BAPI interfaces that were provided by SAP in SAP ERP—do they still exist in SAP S/4HANA? If the data model and the business functions were changed with SAP S/4HANA, we cannot assume that we will find all previous BAPI and RFM interfaces from SAP ERP again in SAP S/4HANA. Some may have vanished, some may have incompatible changes.

Indeed, some RFMs from SAP ERP are *blacklisted* in SAP S/4HANA. Blacklisted means that they exist technically, but the ABAP runtime prevents you calling them. The reason for an RFM to be on the blacklist may be an application development decision or because of incompatible changes in the interface.

SAP Note 2259818 on blacklisted RFMs

 SAP Note 2259818 lists the blacklisted RFMs and provides background information on them. The PDF attached to that note also lists BAPI_MATERIAL_SAVEDATA, which we used in Section 2.5.

You can consult SAP with a support incident to clarify whether a specific RFM can be removed from the blacklist if the customer confirms that all consumers are adapted to the new interface.

One specific topic in the Simplification List is important to mention, as it involves a change in the DDIC which especially affects interfaces. The length of the material number field has been extended from 18 to 40 characters. The respective *Simplification Item* in the Simplification List is *Material Number Field Length Extension*, in which especially the section *The Material Number in Released External Interfaces* is relevant for further details.

This extended material number functionality must be switched on explicitly, either after the installation of the SAP S/4HANA system or after the system conversion from SAP ERP to SAP S/4HANA. It may also affect custom code, which must be adapted after the system conversion.

A new field was added to the interfaces that use the material number field, using the new length of 40 characters. As long as the extended material number functionality is not (yet) switched on, the interfaces still behave in the old way, using the shorter version of the extended field for incoming and outgoing communication. Once the switch has been executed, only the long version can be used. Note that for internal calls of such an interface, the system always uses the long version of these fields. We recommend that you study the description of this simplification item thoroughly. And it is possible that other fields will be extended in SAP S/4HANA in the future.

The fact that some existing interfaces were changed such that they are incompatible with SAP S/4HANA is also the reason why the configuration of an RFC destination which uses fast serialization considers an SAP S/4HANA target system separately (discussed in Section 1.29).

For any RFC destination that involves SAP S/4HANA—either as the client or as the server—the recommendation is to use fast serialization. Fast serialization is recommended even for communication between different releases of SAP S/4HANA because changes in the Data Dictionary can potentially happen in newer SAP S/4HANA releases.

The choice of fast serialization not only offers better performance but also allows more appropriate handling of interface mismatch. It is even possible that in the future, RFC destinations using fast serialization will be able to handle incompatibilities in parameter field lengths (between the client and server side) more intelligently—in some cases even without loss of content. This requires that in the RFC destination, the option CLIENT OR SERVER IS S/4HANA SYSTEM is set appropriately as part of the interface check, as discussed in Section 1.29.

As a final remark, *SAP BW/4HANA* is also based exclusively on the SAP HANA database, just like SAP S/4HANA. Adaptations of the data model are part of this new product line as well.

Custom ABAP development is done in SAP ERP and SAP S/4HANA, and rarely in SAP BW and SAP BW/4HANA. If you do plan to do ABAP development in SAP BW/4HANA, you should check the Simplification List for SAP BW/4HANA.

SAP BW/4HANA Simplification List

 You can view the Simplification List for SAP BW/4HANA on the SAP Help Portal:

https://help.sap.com/viewer/p/SAP_BW4HANA.

For an introduction to SAP BW and SAP BW/4HANA, see the book *SAP BW/4HANA and BW on HANA* (2nd edition, Klaus-Peter Sauer, Frank Riesner, Espresso Tutorials 2017).

ESPRESSO TUTORIALS

You have finished the book.

A The Author

Dr. Boris Rubarth has been gathering experience with SAP software since 1999. He started as an ABAP instructor for customer training at SAP Germany, subsequently specializing in connectivity and integration. He was also responsible for creating a series of SAP training curricula. Boris now works as a Product Manager at SAP SE and lectures at various colleges on ABAP, SAP Basis technology, and SAP Process Integration. He studied Physics in Hamburg and Hanover and received his PhD in Physics in Oldenburg.

B Index

S

SAP BC flow 232
SAP BW/4HANA 240
SAP Connectors 231
   SAP Business Connector 232
   SAP Connector for Microsoft
      .NET 235
   SAP Java Connector (JCo) 233
   SAP NetWeaver RFC Library
      233
SAP Gateway 34
SAP HANA database 237
SAP S/4HANA 237
Secure network communication
   (SNC) 20
Serialization 115
   basXML 118
   basXML forced 120
   Fast serialization 121
   XRFC 117
Simplification Item 239
Simplification List 238
Stable interface 144
Suite-on-HANA (SoH) 237
Supervisor destination 71
Synchronous RFC (sRFC) 62

T

Table appends 148
Terminal ID 32
TEST_RUN parameter 169
Transaction ID 107
Transactional RFC (tRFC) 108
Transfer protocol 116
Trusting/trusted RFC connection
   20

U

Unified Connectivity (UCON) 22
Update function module 77

V

Versioning a BAPI 144
Versioning an interface 111

W

Wrapper RFM 110

X

X structure for BAPI 138

C Disclaimer

This publication contains references to the products of SAP SE.

SAP, R/3, SAP NetWeaver, Duet, PartnerEdge, ByDesign, SAP BusinessObjects Explorer, StreamWork, and other SAP products and services mentioned herein as well as their respective logos are trademarks or registered trademarks of SAP SE in Germany and other countries.

Business Objects and the Business Objects logo, BusinessObjects, Crystal Reports, Crystal Decisions, Web Intelligence, Xcelsius, and other Business Objects products and services mentioned herein as well as their respective logos are trademarks or registered trademarks of Business Objects Software Ltd. Business Objects is an SAP company.

Sybase and Adaptive Server, iAnywhere, Sybase 365, SQL Anywhere, and other Sybase products and services mentioned herein as well as their respective logos are trademarks or registered trademarks of Sybase, Inc. Sybase is an SAP company.

SAP SE is neither the author nor the publisher of this publication and is not responsible for its content. SAP Group shall not be liable for errors or omissions with respect to the materials. The only warranties for SAP Group products and services are those that are set forth in the express warranty statements accompanying such products and services, if any. Nothing herein should be construed as constituting an additional warranty.

More Espresso Tutorials Books

Jelena Perfiljeva:

What on Earth is an SAP® IDoc?

▶ Fundamentals of inbound and outbound IDoc interfaces and configuration

▶ Learn how to implement interfaces with ALE and EDI

▶ Troubleshoot common post-implementation challenges

▶ Quick reference guide to common IDoc transaction codes and reports

http://5130.espresso-tutorials.com

Michal Krawczyk:

SAP® SOA Integration – Enterprise Service Monitoring

▶ Tools for Monitoring SOA Scenarios

▶ Forward Error Handling (FEH) and Error Conflict Handler (ECH)

▶ Configuration Tips

▶ SAP Application Interface Framework (AIF) Customization Best Practices

▶ Detailed Message Monitoring and Reprocessing Examples

http://5077.espresso-tutorials.com

Tom Zamir:

Using SAP® BRFplus in Big Data Scenarios

- ▶ Using BRFplus in a single run scenario
- ▶ Designing BRFplus rules for mass execution
- ▶ Monitoring BRFplus with the SAP Application Interface Framework
- ▶ Leveraging analytic mode in SAP HANA Rules Framework

http://5256.espresso-tutorials.com

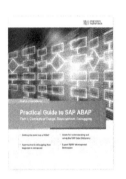

Thomas Stutenbäumer:

Practical Guide to ABAP®. Part 1: Conceptual Design, Development, Debugging

- ▶ How to get the most out of SAP ABAP
- ▶ Guide for understanding and using the SAP Data Dictionary
- ▶ Beginner and advanced debugging techniques
- ▶ Expert ABAP development techniques

http://5121.espresso-tutorials.com

Thomas Stutenbäumer:

Practical Guide to ABAP®. Part 2: Performance, Enhancements, Transports

- ▶ Developer influence on performance
- ▶ Modifications and enhancements to SAP standard
- ▶ SAP access and account management techniques
- ▶ SAP Transport Management System

http://5138.espresso-tutorials.com